ESSAYS ON THE AMERICAN WEST

THE WALTER PRESCOTT WEBB MEMORIAL LECTURES: III

THE WALTER PRESCOTT WEBB MEMORIAL LECTURES

ESSAYS ON THE AMERICAN WEST

BY
SANDRA L. MYRES
BLAINE T. WILLIAMS
ROBERT L. WILLIAMSON
RAY A. BILLINGTON

Introduction by Otis A. Singletary

Edited by
Harold M. Hollingsworth
and Sandra L. Myres

PUBLISHED FOR THE UNIVERSITY OF TEXAS AT ARLINGTON
BY THE UNIVERSITY OF TEXAS PRESS, AUSTIN AND LONDON

Standard Book Number 292-70017-2
Library of Congress Catalog Card Number 77-98406
© 1969 by The University of Texas at Arlington
All Rights Reserved
Type set by G&S Typesetters, Austin
Printed by The University of Texas Printing Division, Austin
Bound by Universal Bookbindery, Inc., San Antonio

PREFACE

The third series of the Walter Prescott Webb Memorial Lectures was held April 16, 1968, in Texas Hall of The University of Texas at Arlington. Departing slightly from the previous pattern, three of the lectures were by members of the faculty at Arlington, Sandra L. Myres, Robert L. Williamson, and Blaine T. Williams, while the fourth was delivered by a distinguished visiting historian, Ray A. Billington. Dr. Billington, who recently has been involved in writing a biography of Frederick Jackson Turner, took this occasion to note the similarities in background, training, and personality that set Webb and Turner apart from the journeyman practitioners of the art of historical writing.

Perhaps the preface to this volume on the American West is an appropriate place to note that Walter P. Webb was not a Western historian per se. He was born in Texas and educated in Texas, but his mind ranged freely over both time and space. *The Great Plains* was not so much a study of the West as a discussion of the impact of geography on the tools and institutions that shape men's lives. *The Great Frontier* looked at the total sweep of Western civilization. Webb associated the opening of free good virgin lands with the development of democracy, free enterprise, voluntarism in religion, and individual rights before the law. It was only in his last years that Webb undertook to write a book on the American West, but he gave it up and published an essay in *Harper's Magazine*, "The American West, Perpetual Mirage," which immediately aroused the ire of politicians and professional Westerners from Denver to Washington.

The Webb Lectures are dedicated to the memory of Walter Prescott Webb, the universal historian. Like him, they are not limited to the West or the South, or even the Americas. They seek to honor his memory by boldly seeking to understand historical processes without regard to time or place. We can only hope that he would be pleased by the results.

HAROLD M. HOLLINGSWORTH
SANDRA L. MYRES

CONTENTS

CONTENTS

INTRODUCTION

It is a tribute to the good will, as well as to the good sense, of the faculty of The University of Texas at Arlington that they chose to establish and support a lecture series in memory of Walter Prescott Webb, for in thus honoring Webb they were voicing not only their admiration for an accomplished professional, but also their deep affection for a long-time friend. Webb *knew* Arlington, and he had a special feeling for the place and the people. It is a matter of record that E. E. Davis was once Webb's roommate and that Joe B. Preston was one of his earliest graduate students. E. C. Barksdale, who is in a good position to know, claims that "no other man has meant so much to the development of the Arlington History Department as has W. P. Webb." These numerous and close personal ties make it all the more fitting that these annual lectures were the brainchild of the Arlington historians.

Begun in the spring of 1966, the Webb Memorial Lectures have from the beginning served the double purpose of bringing distinguished historians to the campus and providing an opportunity to display local campus talent. The first lectures centered around the theme of the American Civil War, and the featured speaker was Frank E. Vandiver, the genial Rice University professor who, had he lived in the eighteen sixties rather than the nineteen sixties and campaigned as hard as he does now, might

just possibly have altered the outcome of the conflict. Homer
Kerr and Martin Hall ably represented the Arlington faculty in
those first lectures. A year later, in April, 1967, the second series
of lectures, focusing upon the New Deal, was delivered by
George Wolfskill and Wilmon Droze of Arlington and featured
William E. Leuchtenburg of Columbia University. The third
Webb lectures were held in April, 1968, and are now published
in this slender volume entitled *Essays on the American West*.

Anyone who knew Webb could tell you that this topic would
have been especially pleasing to him. The American West was
not only an identifiable place to him, it was also a sort of intellectual happy-hunting-ground for his restless, probing mind.
(His article in *Harper's Magazine* on the American West was a
superb piece of writing and I, for one, am sorry that he never
found the time to fully develop that idea into the really significant book I think it would have been.) In addition to being
pleased with the general theme, he would also have appreciated
the individual presentations dealing so well with various aspects
of that frontier that was so much an object of his intellectual
curiosity.

The ranching frontier is the subject of the paper by Sandra L.
Myres of the Arlington History Department. It is her thesis that
one must look south toward the Spanish borderlands rather than
east toward the Appalachians to discover the origins of the institution of ranching. The Anglos adopted the techniques, equipment, mores, and folklore of the Spanish ranchers, and what was
to become known as the cattle kingdom in post–Civil War
America was merely the reappearance of the Spanish ranching
frontier modified and adapted to new circumstances. The animals

themselves were brought to the New World by the conquistadors, as was the mounted herdsman. Branding, guilds (associations), laws and ordinances, riding equipment (Western saddle, lariat), dress (hat, boots, spurs, chaps), and the colorful vocabulary of the cowboy were all to some degree derived from the Spanish ranchers, as were those "twin spectacles of the range," the roundup and the long drive. Professor Myres sees the ranch as a "weapon for the conquest and taming of the frontier," a tool for its settlement and exploitation. In her view, it was the ranch that made the plains not only habitable, but also productive and profitable; it was also the "only Spanish frontier institution to survive intact into the modern age."

"The Frontier Family: Demographic Fact and Historical Myth," by Blaine T. Williams, is a sociological study of "who" had moved into central Texas by the time of the 1850 census. Using statistical data, Williams came to the following conclusions about pioneer families living in the Peters Colony area:

"Land" was the magic word that brought the settlers from the eastern tidelands and the Ohio Valley.

The "marriage at early age" myth did not hold up under careful investigation.

There were significant numbers of unmarried adults, as well as a large number of widows.

Heads of households were in the 20–39 "prime of life" age group.

Settlers tended to import their own kin into the settlement. Professor Williams argues that the frontier family was the "unifying force" in the great migration onto the plains.

In his article on the muzzle-loading rifle, Robert L. Williamson of the Arlington History Department describes it as a "frontier tool." Interestingly enough, it was *not* basically a military weapon; it was not designed for use on horseback or against a mounted foe. Its real importance in frontier life stemmed from the fact that it was essential to daily living; it was a "tool designed for harvesting game." In addition to feeding the frontiersman, the rifle also provided his clothing, his recreation, and his spending money.

The major address in the third lecture series was delivered by Ray A. Billington, senior research associate of the Huntington Library, who is widely known and highly respected for his work in American history. In a most interesting comparison of Webb and Frederick Jackson Turner, Billington underscores many similarities. Both were influenced by the primitive environment in which they were reared and "translated into theory a world with which they were all too familiar." Neither received significant training in the area of his specialty. Turner took only one course in American history, and Webb always claimed to have been ideally prepared for his work because he never had a course in western United States history. Both had enthusiasm for their subject and held a strong, fundamental belief in the importance of the study of history. Neither was a prolific writer, by contemporary standards, and there is some reason to believe that both might have ended up as tenured associate professors in today's marketplace. While neither was a methodical writer, both were steady workers. Both wrote analytical rather than narrative history and preferred to explore not *what* men did, but *why* they did it. Neither was afraid of his own insights; both transcended the narrow confines of their discipline. Both were bitterly attacked. (In Turner's case, the assault on his theory came after his death;

Webb, on the other hand, incurred the wrath of narrow career-
ists during his lifetime.) Both were artists, not just historians.
They were creative and original men who worked in a field
dominated by "traditionalists."

In a final comment on Webb, Billington states his own belief
that *The Great Plains* will continue to be read with appreciation
and that *The Great Frontier* will come to be recognized as "one
of the most significant books of our time." I could not agree
more wholeheartedly.

Billington's words about Webb stirred some pleasant remem-
brances of my own relatively brief relationship with the man. I
do not pretend to be any kind of "inside dopester"; there were
and are many persons around who knew him longer and better
than I. But what I knew about him I liked immensely, and during
those seven years when it was my good fortune to be what I shall
loosely describe as a "colleague" of his, I came to look upon his
friendship as the most tangible fringe benefit to come my way.
During those years, I visited him often in the cluttered office in
Garrison Hall, drank my share of coffee with him in the Union,
audited his course, "The Great Frontier," enjoyed late-hour con-
versations at the Headliners Club, traveled with him from time
to time, and was a fairly frequent companion on visits to Friday
Mountain. As a result of these pleasant experiences, I came to
know and appreciate some of his many moods. He was a quiet
man, but he enjoyed and practiced the civilized art of conversation. He was a kind and gentle man, but there was a directness
about him that could be unsettling. He was a serious man, but
he possessed a streak of wry humor that was at times irrepressible.

I am told, and I would like to think it is true, that Webb had something to do with the job offer that brought me to The University of Texas in 1954. But be that as it may, I shall always remember with gratitude that remarkable man in whose being was reflected to an extraordinary degree independence of spirit, originality of mind, and authenticity of character.

Otis A. Singletary

ESSAYS ON THE AMERICAN WEST

THE RANCHING FRONTIER

Spanish Institutional Backgrounds of the Plains Cattle Industry

BY SANDRA L. MYRES

"ONE OF THE MARVELS in the history of the modern world is the way in which that little Iberian nation, Spain, when most of her blood and treasure were absorbed in European wars, with a handful of men took possession of the Caribbean archipelago, and by rapid yet steady advance spread her culture, her religion, her law, and her language over more than half of the two American continents where they still are dominant and still are secure —in South America, Central America, and a large fraction of North America. . . ."[1]

With these words, Herbert Eugene Bolton began his famous essay on the mission as a frontier institution. Bolton believed that Spain's success in colonizing a vast New World reflected the vigor and virility of her frontier institutions. To illustrate this thesis, he contributed valuable studies of the presidio and mission, fron-

[1] Herbert Eugene Bolton, "The Mission as a Frontier Institution in the Spanish American Colonies," *American Historical Review*, XXIII (October, 1917), 42.

tier agencies that helped to establish and extend Spanish military, political, and religious control beyond the boundaries of pacified and settled areas.

The Spaniards also utilized the ranch as a frontier institution. Like the mission and the presidio, the ranch was a multifaceted, multipurpose pioneering agency with economic, political, social, and cultural features. Long before the discovery of America, the effectiveness of pastoral establishments as a means of securing, holding, and developing large tracts of semiarid land had been tested along the Moorish-Iberian frontiers on the Mesa Central of Spain. Afterwards, as the Spaniards moved out from the Caribbean Islands onto the continent and northward into New Mexico, Texas, Arizona, and California, ranchers, accompanied by their flocks and herds, took their own place beside the soldiers and churchmen in the forefront of Spanish advance.

Unlike the mission and presidio, the ranch did not disappear with the passing of the Spanish frontier and the coming of Anglo-Americans to the Southwest. Instead the Anglos adopted the techniques, equipment, even the mores and folklore of the Spanish ranchers. The ranching frontier reappeared, modified and adapted to new circumstances, but basically intact, in the post–Civil War American West. The Anglo-American ranching kingdom not only contributed to the opening and taming of the West, but it also became famous as a unique development peculiarly adapted to the needs of the frontier. Furthermore, the Western ranch was different from any similar institution east of the Mississippi. Even today, the history, literature, economics, and politics of the Anglo cattle kingdom remain a source of interest and study for scholars and laymen seeking to explain the development of the westward movement. Yet if we are to understand the genesis of this institution, we must look not eastward toward the Appalachians but southward toward the Spanish borderlands. For it was here, in the areas conquered and pacified by Spain, that the cattle kingdom had its roots. It was the Spaniards who introduced the first animals, developed the techniques for working vast herds, and established the basis for widespread and profitable pastoral industries in the New World.

During the first decades of Spanish conquest, the livestock, organization, methods, and customs of the Iberian ranching system reached the Indies and became the foundation of all American ranching. Christopher Columbus brought the first animals to Santo Domingo. They multiplied rapidly, and soon the Caribbean Islands supported numerous stock farms that provided the basis for a self-sustaining economy. Island ranches also furnished the meat and animals necessary for the conquest of the mainland. Sheep, cattle, horses, and hogs accompanied the conquistadors from the Indies into Panama, Mexico, Peru, and later northward and southward into all the lands of Spanish America.

Historians have frequently misunderstood or misinterpreted the documents relating to the progenitors of the famous Longhorn cattle of North America. The cows the Spaniards imported to their overseas colonies constituted a breed unique in both Europe and colonial America. These animals varied in color from yellows and duns to deep browns, reds, and blacks. They were distinguished by their long, low-swinging heads, formidable horns, narrow sides, and long legs. The Spanish cattle, unsuited for dairy or draft purposes, were valued chiefly for their tough hides and stringy beef, and they were perfectly adapted to a frontier existence. They were tough, strong stock, characterized by marked feral instincts and often complete wildness. They were able to survive and maintain themselves in country that would have decimated or destroyed herds of weaker and less self-sufficient animals. Conditioned to the semiarid plains of Castile, accustomed to roam untended and uncared for from roundup to roundup, the Spanish cattle made perfect specimens to survive in the unpopulated areas of the Americas—from the pampas of Argentina to the plains of Texas.

These animals were not the famous black cattle (*ganado prieto*), which were carefully bred, nurtured, and trained for the bull ring. Some black cattle were raised in the New World, and some were even introduced into the northern borderlands, but they never constituted more than a single small branch in the family tree of the North American range cow. The Spanish cattle that went into northern Mexico with Ibarra and Rodríquez, into New Mexico with Coronado and Oñate, into Texas with Alonso de León and Escandón, and later up the trail to Kansas with the Texas cowboys were the hybrid result of centuries of selection by survival, a breed developed by and for frontier conditions.

Although in other pastoral industries, notably in raising sheep and horses, the Spaniards introduced new bloodlines and attempted to upgrade their stock, they allowed the range cattle to remain unchanged until the late nineteenth century. The Spanish rancher found his tough, stringy animals remarkably well suited to the frontier environment, and he did little or nothing to improve the quality of his stock. This is not really surprising when one remembers that the Anglo cowmen did little to upgrade their herds until the introduction of Shorthorn and Hereford bulls in the late 1870's. Selective breeding practices could not become widespread until the end of the frontier period, when ranching gave way to stock farming. Only when free grass was exhausted and the open range was closed did ranchers build fenced pastures and corrals where breeding selection could be carefully supervised and controlled.

The Spaniards provided the livestock necessary for the establishment of pastoral industries, and they also developed the equipment and techniques essential to ranching. Cattle and other livestock were raised almost everywhere in Europe and America, but it is important to note that cattle raising and cattle ranching are *not* the same thing. As Charles Bishko pointed out in his study of peninsular stock raising, ranching "implies the ranging of cattle in considerable numbers over extensive grazing grounds for the primary purpose of large scale production of beef and hides."[2] Ranching was an extensive productive enterprise, and it required larger tracts of pasture land and different methods than did the care of a few dairy cows and small herds as an adjunct to agriculture. During the Middle Ages, cattle ranching in western Europe was confined to the Iberian Peninsula. The ranching techniques developed in Spain were transplanted to the Western Hemisphere, where they were modified to meet new conditions imposed by the vast grasslands and sparse population of the North American plains. A few examples will show the Spanish impact on American ranching.

One of the most distinctive features of Spanish ranching was the mounted herdsman. Even before the conquest of the New World, the Spaniards began to carry out most of their ranching activities from horseback. This custom was continued and refined

[2] Charles J. Bishko, "The Peninsular Background of Latin American Cattle Ranching," *Hispanic American Historical Review*, XXXIII (November, 1952), 494.

on the American plains. On the other hand, French and English herders were rarely mounted. East of the Appalachians, English colonial stock raisers usually worked their herds on foot, sometimes with the aid of well-trained sheep or cattle dogs. When the Anglo stockman crossed the Mississippi and ventured onto the plains, he discovered that the long distances he had to travel and the mean, cantankerous nature of stock raised on open range required that he copy the Spanish ranching methods.

When the Anglo learned to work cattle from horseback, he also borrowed Spanish riding equipment. Since the Spaniards were mounted herdsmen, it is not surprising that the basic tool of the range industry—the Western stock saddle—was modeled on Spanish prototypes. Each part of the Spanish work saddle or *silla de campo* was designed to aid the vaquero in his ranching chores. The curved cantle and long stirrups provided a comfortable seat for the rider during long hours in the saddle. The high pommel and thick, strong horn served as a roping post and gave additional stability to the horseman. The large, flat Spanish stirrups furnished a firm foothold for the rider chasing cattle across the countryside.

In addition to copying the Spanish saddle and claiming it as his own, the Anglo cowboy also borrowed the *reata* or lariat, a braided rope used to catch and tie cattle and other livestock. Spanish herdsmen experimented with several techniques before they learned the best method for roping the large wild cattle of the American plains. At first the vaqueros tied the end of the lariat to the horse's tail, but they quickly realized that for roping wild cattle the tail rope was both awkward and dangerous. They therefore transferred the lariat to the pommel of the saddle. After throwing his loop, the rider wrapped his rope around the saddle horn, secured the animal, and allowed the saddle to absorb the weight and pull of the captured bull or cow. In Spanish this method of roping was called *da la vuelta*. When the Anglos learned the technique, they shortened and corrupted the Spanish phrase and called it "dally" roping. Some Anglos learned to dally, but many a novice cowhand lacked the necessary speed and dexterity to make fast his rope and still get his hand free of the rope and saddle horn. Most Anglos preferred to tie-fast. They secured the lariat to the saddle with a "tie" or knot. This Anglo system of roping was not as flashy or skillful a procedure as the dally, but it did prevent a generation of Texas cowboys from going through life minus a thumb. Mexican vaqueros continued to dally, however, and their skill in using the lariat to bring down wild stock was a constant source of amazement and admiration to visitors on Spanish-American ranches.

In addition to roping skills, other Spanish ranching methods became common throughout the Americas. Essential to working large numbers of livestock were the roundup and the drive, techniques that Walter Prescott Webb termed the "twin spectacles of the range."[3] Both the roundup and the drive were perfected by the Spanish *ganaderos* ("cowmen") long before the first Texas cowboy ever tossed a rope over a Longhorn steer. As Webb noted, the roundup was to cattle what the harvest is to wheat, "a gathering of the products of the Plains grass."[4] It was invented to facilitate the sorting of herds that had become mixed on the common pastures and to bring in young stock. The mounted cowhands fanned out in a circle and drove the cattle toward some

[3] Walter Prescott Webb, *The Great Plains* (New York: Grosset and Dunlap, 1957), p. 255.
[4] Ibid.

previously designated central point. There they sorted the cattle according to their brands. Strays or *mostrencos* were turned over to the king's representatives as property of the royal domain. Unbranded animals or *orejanos* were divided among the stockmen.

Spanish laws regulating the livestock industry specified that roundups must be held weekly between the middle of June and the end of November, but there were frequent violations of the rule. In the northern borderlands, Indian raids and unpredictable climate often made weekly roundups impractical. Therefore the Spanish ranchers—and later the Anglos—organized one or two big roundups a year, usually in the spring and fall.

Unfortunately, we have few descriptions of roundups in the Spanish Southwest. Evidently the practice was so common and the procedure so familiar that Spaniards saw no need to explain it. The few descriptions we do have, principally from the journals of foreign travelers, make it clear that the techniques used during the seventeenth and eighteenth centuries were surprisingly similar to those employed by Mexican and Anglo ranchers in the late nineteenth and early twentieth centuries. It is interesting to picture the scene that occurred on the Texas plains in 1788 when missionaries and ranchers combined forces to round up the unbranded stock in the pastures south of San Antonio. Imagine blue-robed Franciscans, cassocks flapping in the breeze; half-clothed Indian herdsmen crouched over the necks of sturdy mustangs; Spanish rancheros, attired in the long leather coats and *botas de ala* ("leggings") typical of the eighteenth-century cowman—all attempting to chase down and brand wild cattle that roamed free and unrestricted over the open countryside.

Spanish ranchers also perfected techniques for moving large

numbers of livestock from one place to another. In Spain, sharp contrasts in climate and topography made semiannual changes in grazing lands desirable. Long before coming to the Western Hemisphere, the Iberian herdsmen worked out methods for livestock migration that included a system of communal livestock trails and seasonal pastures. In the New World, too, changing pasture conditions and distant market centers required transmigration of herds and flocks, and peninsular practices were transferred to the Spanish colonies. Throughout the Americas, Spanish ranchers shifted their herds from one grazing area to another. They also took their animals to market "on the hoof," driving them hundreds of miles to fairs, slaughtering pens, and distribution points. The Spanish livestock trade was not so well publicized as the "rivers of beef" that flowed northward out of Texas after the Civil War. Nonetheless, the Spaniards did build up an extensive commerce and perfected the methods and equipment used by the Texas cowboys along the trail to Abilene.

Cattle driving posed a number of problems. Because the Spaniards rarely castrated their stock, they faced the unenviable task of moving large herds of bulls. Spanish ranchers, therefore, relied on trained oxen to tame the cattle and break them to the trail. The vaqueros used a hair rope or halter called a *cabresto* to harness the bulls to the oxen. These huge, plodding beasts patiently led—or dragged—the recalcitrant bulls until they were broken to the trail. Although Anglo cowmen rarely employed the *cabresto*, they frequently used a lead ox or steer on drives. Both Spanish and Anglo ranchers used trained oxen to bring cattle in from the open range.

Another problem arose during livestock migrations. Herds overran plowed and planted fields and caused extensive damage

to crops. This brought forth loud protests from the farmers who
retaliated by slaughtering stray animals and selling the meat in
local markets. In some areas, settlers claimed the migratory herds
were more dangerous to life and property than unpacified Indian
tribes. In Texas, citizens of San Fernando de Béxar constantly
complained about loose stock that roamed the streets and fields
of the town. The Spanish viceroys issued a series of regulations
requiring every rancher to provide an adequate guard for his
stock, but the laws were rarely enforced. Such problems were not
very different from those encountered by Texas trail herds in
Kansas and Nebraska during the 1860's and 1870's, and the
Anglos had little more success than the Spaniards in solving
them.

Another important technique utilized by the *ganaderos* was the
identification of livestock by the use of brands and earmarks. In
frontier areas, where animals were rarely kept in fenced en-
closures, herds easily became intermingled and ownership con-
fused. To meet this problem, Spanish ranchers used branding as
a simple and effective means for separating and identifying their
animals. In the Iberian Peninsula, livestock branding was an old
custom dating back to the tenth century, and Iberian sheep and
cattle brands became the antecedents of symbols and monograms
common to ranches throughout the New World.

In the early sixteenth century, cattle bearing the brand of
Hernán Cortés grazed in the Valley of Oaxaca, and a large number of brands owned by early settlers were registered with the
cabildo of Mexico City. To protect brands and regulate their use,
an elaborate code of brand ordinances evolved. The laws required
that each stockman have a distinct brand so that his animals
could be easily recognized. Anyone who did not have a ranch

could not have a branding iron, nor was he permitted to mark stock in any way. Later, ranchers were assigned two brands. One was the permanent range brand (*el fierro para herrar los ganados*) burned into the animal's hide with a hot iron. The second was a sale brand (*el fierro para ventear*) similar to the Anglo-American trail brand. This second mark was usually applied with pitch or other temporary substances, and it was used only at the time of sale or in moving livestock from pasture to market. Numerous laws were enacted in an attempt to discourage thefts, brand alterations, and mavericking. Other ordinances regulated hide hunting, slaughtering, the semiannual roundups, and the use of common pasture and grazing land.

Enforcement of these various ordinances was necessary to the orderly regulation of ranching. This function was carried out by the Mesta—a quasi-governmental organization with responsibility for both formulation and enforcement of livestock laws. Soon after the conquest, the *cabildo* of Mexico City and the leading stockmen of the area established the Mexican Mesta or stockowner's guild. The primary purpose of the Mesta was to further the interests of the ranchers and to deal with problems associated with the rapid growth of the livestock industry. Alcaldes de Mesta were appointed to assign and register brands, supervise roundups, enforce the livestock laws, and adjudicate disputes between cattle and sheep owners. As ranching expanded northward and the pastoral industries increased in importance, new livestock regulations were included in the codes, and additional officials were appointed to enforce them. In many borderlands areas, Mesta officers served as itinerant justices of the peace with authority to investigate murders, thefts, and other crimes.

Laws and ordinances for the regulation and control of ranch-

ing activities added significantly to the development of Spanish
legal codes. These laws also provided examples for the Anglo-
Americans. Western ranchmen of the nineteenth century borrowed liberally from Spanish rules governing branding, slaughtering, and grazing rights; and the Mesta served as a pattern for
the powerful stockmen's associations of the trans-Mississippi
West.

Spanish ranchers added a colorful and romantic chapter to the
history of the Americas. The distinctive dress of the modern
cowboy—big hat, boots, spurs, chaps—still reflects the clothing
designed by the vaqueros to aid them in their work. Ranching
terms such as reata, dally, vaquero, and rodeo enrich the Spanish
and English vocabulary. The games and sports of the West are
based on ranching practices. Fiestas still feature demonstrations
of proficiency with lasso and horse, and the professional rodeo as
a form of competitive sport and entertainment is based on the
skills and abilities of the cowboy.

Far more important than the strictly technical and social aspects of ranching was the use of the ranch as a frontier institution. Throughout the Americas, ranching served as an effective
tool for the settlement and exploitation of frontier areas. Unlike
the English, the Spaniards had considerable frontier experience
before coming to the Western Hemisphere. They had experimented with various institutions to hold and control frontier
areas in medieval Spain, and they transferred many of these
agencies to the New World, adapting and modifying them to
meet the conditions they found. Thus the frontier fortresses of
the Iberian Peninsula became the presidial garrisons of the northern borderlands, the Church modified its methods for conversion

and established the mission system, and the ranch became an institution for economic and political development.

In many parts of the New World, opportunities for economic growth were severely limited. For example, in northern Mexico and the southwestern United States, the Spaniards found the flat, semiarid grassland poorly suited to agriculture. Mineral resources were largely undiscovered or unexploitable. Yet the Spaniards, accustomed to the dry plains of Castile, understood the geographical limitations of the region. They quickly adapted to the conditions of climate and topography that they found, and they turned to ranching as a means for utilizing the available natural resources. Cattle, horses, and the by-products of the ranching industry furnished food, tallow, and leather, thus providing a livelihood for those pioneers willing to endure the hardships of frontier life.

In many places, ranching constituted the major economic activity of the settlers. Those who came, or were sent, to the far-flung outposts of Empire along New Spain's northern borders had little to invest. The Indians were difficult to civilize, and labor was scarce. Ranching offered a partial solution to these problems. With a few animals for breeding stock and access to grazing land, the rancher was in business. The half-wild Spanish stock required little care, and throughout the Southwest the frontier ranchers became owners of huge herds and masters of seemingly interminable stretches of grassland.

To aid ranching development, the Spanish monarchs issued land grants that recognized the need of the livestock industry for large tracts of pasture and grazing lands. In determining the size of land grants, the Anglo thought in terms of acres. The Spaniard thought in terms of land utilization, and Spanish land grants reflected either agricultural or pastoral use. In Spanish America, land suitable for irrigation and farming was divided into small units called *labores*. Like the Anglo quarter section, the *labor* was intended as a land unit sufficient to produce food crops for a single family. Grasslands were alloted in blocks large enough to provide adequate grazing for livestock. The *sitio de ganado menor*, a grant of approximately 2,000 acres, was used for raising sheep, goats, and other small animals. A more extensive tract, the *sitio de ganado mayor* or league, was designed for large animals, such as cattle and horses. The league varied in size from 4,300 to 4,500 acres.

Throughout the Spanish colonies, livestock owners frequently received three or four leagues of land, and it was not uncommon for them to acquire or lease additional acreage. Some ranchers put together vast landholdings based on livestock grants. In Texas, for example, Enrique Villareal owned land that included most of the present-day city of Corpus Christi. José Narcisco Cabazos held title to more than 600,000 acres in what are now Cameron, Willacy, and Kenedy counties, and José de la Garza claimed 59.5 leagues of land in the Río Grande Valley.

In addition to individual grants, the Spaniards provided for communal or collective holdings. In ancient times, the towns of Castile owned or controlled extensive territory. These municipal lands included *baldíos* or *dehesas*—vacant pasture and grazing land in the open countryside. Stockmen pastured animals on the *dehesa* under license from the government until such time as the land was granted to an individual. This system was continued in the New World. Throughout the American Southwest, most of the unclaimed grazing land was made available to all stockowners. Hemmed in by restrictions imposed by Eastern legis-latures, the Anglo, like his Spanish predecessor, turned to this open range or free grass in order to obtain sufficient forage for large-scale ranching activities. On both the Spanish and Anglo frontiers, common pasture provided grass for large herds of livestock on the semiarid plains, while the river valleys and well-watered areas were reserved for farming and agriculture.

Ranching did not always dominate the economic life of the borderlands. In many places, Hispanic-American frontier de-velopment followed the pattern later outlined by Frederick Jack-son Turner for the Anglo-American West: exploration, mining, ranching—each frontier served as guide and stimulus to the next. Gold and silver rushes in nineteenth-century Colorado, Nevada, and Montana resembled earlier mining ventures in sixteenth-century New Spain, where the discovery of mineral resources attracted ranching enterprises for the support of the camps and towns. Not all stockmen, of course, responded to the lure of easy riches and new markets. Great ranches developed in areas of Mexico that were completely lacking in mines. In the United States, much of the cattle country was not mining country—for example, Kansas, Nebraska, Oklahoma, and the Texas Pan-handle. At the same time, the symbiotic relationship between mining and ranching on both the Spanish and Anglo-American frontiers should not be overlooked.

In northern New Spain, the livestock industry usually ex-panded in conjunction with the advance of the mining frontier. Wherever mines opened, towns grew up, and the demand for meat, hides, and tallow increased. Soon large ranches or *estancias* appeared throughout the mining districts. For instance, in 1564, reports from Nombre de Dios showed 250,000 head of sheep and cattle grazing on the pasture lands surrounding the mines, and the number in other areas was much the same.

Ranching not only supported mining and other industries, but it also helped sustain Spanish imperial policy throughout the frontier regions. Although not designed as political or religious institutions, the ranches contributed to the development of the presidios and missions in their attempts to conquer, convert, and civilize the American Indian. Political and economic control of the natives was essential to Spanish expansion in the New World. Hindered by a relatively small population, numerous European commitments, and a vast area to dominate, Spaniards felt they must exploit the Amerindian, Hispanicize him, and make him a useful, productive laborer. This was fairly easy among the civilized tribes of Mexico and Peru, but, on the frontiers, this obligation—undertaken primarily by the missionaries and military commanders—was more difficult.

Ranching proved to be an important complement to the work of conversion by enabling the Church fathers to offset some of the expenses of mission upkeep through profits derived from ranch products. Every mission from Florida to California had extensive pasture lands stocked with sheep, goats, oxen, horses, and cattle. These animals supplied hides, wool, and tallow for mission industries. The padres taught their charges to tan and weave and to make shoes, harness, candles, and other items for use in the mission or for sale to nearby settlements and garrisons. The ranches furnished meat for the Indian to hunt and eat and thus somewhat lessened the chance he would "take off for the hills" in search of deer, buffalo, and other game. Stock raising also aided in the difficult task of civilizing and Hispanicizing the neophytes. Since the techniques were similar to the chase and hunt, ranching utilized skills the natives already possessed and made it easier for the nomadic Indian to adjust to a new and more sedentary way of life.

In other ways, too, the ranch advanced the work of political expansion and control. Ranching was a valuable asset to the presidios, those tiny outposts of empire charged with responsibility for protecting the borders and holding back the flood of foreign intruders. These frontier fortresses were located in areas far removed from main communication and supply routes. Throughout the colonial period, presidial commanders and provincial governors complained of difficulty in obtaining food, clothing, and equipment. The ranchers helped alleviate these shortages by providing not only meat but also oxen for plowing, mules for hauling supplies, and, most important, horses for mounting the presidial troops. On the frontier, mounted men were essential to maintain communications between widely separated points, to patrol the extensive boundaries, and to wage war against the Plains tribes. The horse was necessary to the maintenance of Spanish authority, and local ranches were the main source of supply.

It might be noted that the Anglo-Americans also used the ranch to implement government policy. Unlike the Spaniard, the Anglo did not attempt to exploit or civilize the Amerindian. Rather, the Anglo hoped to eliminate the native or at least to contain and control him. To this end, the United States established a series of Indian reservations. But, as a ward of the government, the Indian had to be fed and cared for, and he had to be kept on the reservation. Western ranches supplied horses for mounting the United States cavalry patrols and also furnished beef for government food issues. Finally, when government aid stopped and farming failed, the reservation Indian turned to ranching in an attempt to wrest a living from the inhospitable plains.

The Spaniards, and later the Anglo-Americans, found the ranch ideally suited to frontier conditions, and they made the ranch a weapon for the conquest and taming of the frontier. The ranchers' migratory wealth could be removed from the raids and incursions of enemies. Ranch products could be transported to market without the use of highly developed or sophisticated transportation facilities. Ranching adapted itself to the lack of both human and natural resources in the sparsely populated area along the frontier. Throughout the Americas—from Argentina to Texas—Spanish frontiersmen left a rich legacy in equipment and techniques for working livestock, in legal codes and stock- men's associations, and in vocabulary and folklore. But, more important, the Spanish ranchers were the first to exploit the American plains and make them not only habitable but also pro- ductive and profitable. In the nineteenth century, Spanish live- stock and ranching techniques spread northward from Texas into the trans-Mississippi West and served to create new fortunes, a new society, a whole new way of life—the legendary Western cattle kingdom. Until the Industrial Revolution provided the tools to bring farming and industry, ranching dominated the economic, political, and cultural life of both the Spanish and Anglo-American West. The ranch outlasted the mission and presidio and became the only Spanish frontier institution to survive intact into the modern age.

Bibliographical Note

In comparison to the hundreds of studies of Anglo-American ranching, little has been written on Spanish-American ranching practices. Most of the material for this essay has been drawn from manuscript records and printed documentary sources. The principal manuscript collections utilized were the Béxar, Laredo, and Saltillo Archives (manuscripts, photostats, transcripts, and microfilm) housed at The University of Texas at Austin. Particularly valuable was a long treatise prepared by the ranchers of San Fernando de Béxar, "Representación que la República de la villa de San Fernando ha puesto a los pies de Rafael Martínez Pachuco," which traces the development of the livestock industry at San Antonio from 1718 to 1787.

Documents relating to the livestock industry of northern Mexico and Spanish Texas and Louisiana are to be found in Herbert Eugene Bolton, ed., *Athanase de Mézières and the Louisiana Texas Frontier, 1768–1780,* 2 vols. (Cleveland: Arthur H. Clark Co., 1914); *Documentos para la historia eclesiástica y civil de la provincia de Texas* (Madrid: Ediciones J. Porrúa Turanzas, 1961); Lawrence Kinnaird, ed., "Spain in the Mississippi Valley, 1765–1794," American Historical Association *Annual Report for 1945,* 3 parts (Washington, D.C.: Government Printing Office, 1946); Pierre Margry, ed., *Découvertes et établissements des français dan l'ouest et dans le sud de l'Amérique Septentrionale, 1614–1754, Mémoires et documents originaux,* 6 vols. (Paris: Impr. D. Jouaust, 1875–1886); and A. B. Thomas, *Teodoro de Croix and the Northern Frontier of New Spain, 1776–1783* (Norman: University of Oklahoma Press, 1941).

Journals, travel accounts, and diaries for the colonial period also contain valuable material, particularly Fray José Francisco López, "The Texas Missions in 1785," translated by J. Autry Dabbs in *Preliminary Studies,* III, No. 6 (Austin: Texas Catholic Historical Society, 1934); Fray Juan Agustín de Morfi, *Diario y derrotero, 1777–1781*, Edición de Eugenio del Hoyo y Malcolm D. McLean (Monterrey: Biblioteca del Instituto Tecnológico de Estudios Superiores de Monterrey, 1967); Morfi, *Viaje de Indios y diario del Nuevo México*, Edición de Vito Alessio Robles (Mexico City: Antigua Librería Robredo de José Porrúa e Hijos, 1935). Descriptions of horse and cattle roundups in the eighteenth century are found in Marie François Pierre de Pagès, *Travels Round the World in the Years 1767, 1768, 1769, 1770, 1771,* 2 vols. (London: J. Murray, 1791), and Donald Jackson, ed., *The Journals of Zebulon Montgomery Pike,* 2 vols. (Norman: University of Oklahoma Press, 1966).

Some secondary sources contain useful information on the development of Spanish ranching methods. For the Iberian backgrounds, see Julius Klein, *The Mesta: A Study in Spanish Economic History, 1274–1836* (Cambridge, Mass.: Harvard University Press, 1920), and Charles J. Bishko, "The Peninsular Background of Latin American Cattle Ranching," *Hispanic American Historical Review,* XXXIII (November, 1952), 491–515. The introduction of Spanish livestock into the Caribbean area is discussed in Carl O. Sauer, *The Early Spanish Main* (Berkeley: University of California Press, 1966). Livestock raising in New Spain (Mexico) is the subject of three authors: Donald D. Brand, "The Early History of the Range Cattle Industry in Northern Mexico," *Agricultural History,* XXXV (July, 1961), 132–139; José Mantesanz, "Introducción de la ganadería en Nueva España, 1521–1535," *Historia Mexicana,* XIV (April, 1964), 522–566; and Richard J. Morrisey, "The Establishment and Northward Expansion of Cattle Ranching in New Spain," Ph.D. thesis, University of California at Berkeley, 1949. The most valuable works on institutional aspects of Mexican colonial ranching are François Chevalier, *Land and Society in Colonial Mexico—the Great Hacienda* (Berkeley: University of California Press, 1963), and William H.

Dusenberry, *The Mexican Mesta: The Administration of Ranching in Colonial Mexico* (Urbana: University of Illinois Press, 1963).

Spanish riding styles and equestrian equipment are discussed in Nicolás Rangel, *Historia del toreo en México, época Colonial, 1529–1821* (Mexico City: Imprenta Manuel León Sánchez, 1924); Juan Suárez de Peralta, *Tratado de la jineta y de la Brida* (Mexico City, 1580; reprint Mexico City: José Álvarez de Villar, 1950); and Arthur Woodward, "Saddles in the New World," *Quarterly of the Los Angeles County Museum*, X (Summer, 1953), 1–5. Leovigildo Islas Escárcega, *Vocabulario campesino nacional, objeciones y ampliaciones al vocabulario agrícola Nacional* (Mexico City: Instituto de Investigaciones Lingüísticas, 1935), is invaluable for definitions of equestrian and ranching terminology and some illustrations of the use of equipment.

Ranching in the Spanish borderlands is briefly discussed by Odie B. Faulk in *The Last Years of Spanish Texas, 1778–1821* (The Hague: Mouton & Co., 1964), and "Ranching in Spanish Texas," *Hispanic American Historical Review*, XLIV (May, 1965), 257–266. LeRoy Graf, "The Economic History of the Lower Río Grande Valley, 1820–1875," 2 vols., Ph.D. thesis, Harvard, 1942, includes a chapter on colonial Spanish ranching practices. A popular writer, Jo Mora, presents some interesting material and illustrations for Spanish California in *Californios: The Saga of the Hard Riding Vaqueros, America's First Cowboys* (Garden City: Doubleday & Co., 1949), and *Trail Dust and Saddle Leather* (New York: Charles Scribner's Sons, 1946), but unfortunately Mora gives no references or bibliography and the authenticity of some of his material is questionable. The introduction of Spanish livestock into Texas and an outline of areas for further research are presented by Sandra L. Myres in "The Spanish Cattle Kingdom in the Province of Texas," *Texana*, IV (Fall, 1966), 233–246.

THE FRONTIER FAMILY

Demographic Fact and Historical Myth

BY BLAINE T. WILLIAMS

ADVENTURE, AMBITION, WANDERLUST, the chance to begin again, and "land for the boys"[1] are but a few of the motives that have been suggested to explain the phenomenon of westward migration. Whatever the impelling forces, until the closing of the frontier, nineteenth-century Americans moved in a series of searches for their own El Dorado.[2] Many chronicles have been written that tell the story of the moves, where they passed by, and the final journey's end.

The presence of Englishmen in Jamestown and Plymouth and Dutchmen in New Amsterdam signaled the opening of the United States land mass to the flood tide of immigration and settlement. A few, very few, came with fame and fortune already secured. Some were indentured servants or convicts, but the

---

[1] Arthur W. Calhoun, *A Social History of the American Family* (New York: Barnes & Noble, Inc., 1960), II, 52.

[2] Ray Allen Billington, *America's Frontier Heritage* (New York: Holt, Rinehart, and Winston, 1966), p. 67.

majority were risktakers looking for the land of beginning again. Until the frontier disappeared, a restless and relentless tide of people swept across the nation in a succession of westward migrations.[3] The early areas of settlement were along the eastern seaboard and tidelands and generally followed the waterways into the hinterland.

For over two hundred years the eastern seaboard and tidelands regions were exposed to land exploitation and overcultivation. Here the power elite, through economic and family ties, produced a social and political structure more secure than that of many of the reigning houses of Europe. Not only were the available lands under the domination of this elite group, but, just as important, class lines rigidly excluded the talented person having neither fortune nor proper ancestors. Class structure and status were ascribed and inherited, with the power passing from father to son or son-in-law. Not only was this closed system effective in the social and economic sense, but it also exerted control over a political system notable for shaping local and national leaders. This was the structure that produced the Washington, Jefferson, Randolph, Madison, Marshall, Rutledge, Carrol, Carter, Pinckney, Butler, and Lee families.

Excluded from the ongoing system was the newcomer, the nonconformist, the innovator, and the individual possessing the ambition but lacking the necessary prerequisite of family. The door to vertical class-mobility was not open to many. Beginning late in the eighteenth century, members of this disadvantaged group created a new wave of immigration that poured over the Appalachians, into the broad Ohio Valley, and eventually onto the central plains. Until 1841, the steady flow of frontier migra-

[3] Calhoun, *History of the American Family*, II, 170.

tion was westward, but at this point in our national history a part
of the pattern was attracted to the Republic of Texas. Free land
served as a magnet and diverted land seekers to the southwest.

On February 4, 1841, a petition by W. S. Peters and nineteen
other men to colonize land in Texas was favorably received by
the Congress of the Republic of Texas. "An Act Granting Land
to Immigrants" was passed, giving the Texas Agricultural, Com-
mercial and Manufacturing Company exclusive rights to offer
free land to settlers in a specified section of north central Texas.[4]
Specifically, the area involved was called the Peters Colony and
included the land mass within the present boundaries of Dallas,
Tarrant, Collin, Denton, Grayson, and Cooke counties. Under
the terms of the contract, the Peters Company was to attract
a stipulated number of settlers to move into the area. The only
persons eligible to receive free land were non-Texans. The Republic wanted an influx of new people, not a rearrangement of
persons already there. Each mature head of household, including
widow or widower with family, was entitled to 640 acres of free
land. An unmarried male, seventeen years of age or over, was to
receive 320 acres.

This study is an analysis of the *who*, not the when, where, or
the how of the Peters Colony. The objects of this study are the
families who moved into north central Texas by the time of the
seventh United States census in 1850.[5] No claim is made that
these data provide universal generalizations about the typical
frontier family. What this study will describe are the characteristics of the pioneer families who lived in the Peters Colony as

---

[4] Seymour V. Connor, *The Peters Colony of Texas* (Austin: The Texas State Historical Association, 1959), Chapters III, IV, and V.

[5] *U.S. Seventh Census, 1850* (MSS., Returns of Schedules I & IV).

of 1850. Numerous other studies must be made before generalizations would be valid concerning the typical frontier family
profile.

The research employed the techniques of demographic analysis. The prime data were gathered from the United States Census
of 1850, Schedules 1 and 4, and the records of the Texas Land
Office. The general inaccuracy of the census of 1850 has been
well documented by Seymour V. Connor and need not be reveri-
fied.[6] Connor estimates that the census is at least a 20-percent
underenumeration. This, however, does not invalidate the data,
since the situation in Texas was quite typical of that to be found
in any emerging frontier situation. A coding technique was employed, using the information on the census and the land patent
information. Thus, it was possible to distinguish nativity, occupation, marital status, and age. Since the census of 1850 was the
first in the so-called modern series, which included personal data
covering state of birth and similar information, it was amenable
to rather sophisticated sociological coding and collating techniques. An individual IBM card was prepared for all families as
well as each single adult and various "sorts" or analyses of the
data were prepared.

What then are the demographic characteristics of the Peters
Colony residents, these seekers for "land for the boys"? The 1850
census lists a total population of 8,414 in the six-county Peters
Colony area. This figure included 113 persons in the military at
Fort Worth, which, when subtracted from the total population,
leaves 8,301 persons who came voluntarily into the area. In this
instance the word *voluntary* needs further qualification, since 591
slaves were involved in the census total. The important factor in

[6] Connor, *Peters Colony*, Chapter XI.

any emerging settlement pattern is the "available adult work force," and slaves were definitely a part of this grouping; therefore, they have been included with the "land seekers" in the total population count. They have been excluded, however, from the analyses discussed below, because such data as marital status, occupation, and nativity were not listed on the census for slaves. Thus, this study deals with a total white, nonmilitary population of 7,710.

Where did these 7,710 people come from? Comparing the state of nativity of the husband and wife yields some insight into migration patterns. Using the techniques employed by Barnes Lathrop[7] and others, it is possible to compare the nativity state of each child with that of the parents, thereby describing a pattern of minimal moves. There may have been moves where no child was born, or instances where a child died and this fact is not shown on the record. However, a father born in North Carolina, who married a girl born in Tennessee, and whose children were born in Illinois, Arkansas, and Texas is known to have made at least three moves, and probably four. Analysis of the data reveals that a total of 648 wives were born in the border South—Arkansas, Missouri, Kentucky, or Tennessee—yet only 407 of them married a man born in the same region. There was obviously a considerable amount of migration going on, since 162 of these women married men born in the South, 52 from the border North, 21 from the North, and 6 of foreign birth.

Some additional information on the flow pattern of migration can be obtained by comparing the state of nativity to the state of residence just prior to removing to Texas. Table 1 represents

[7] Barnes F. Lathrop, *Migration into East Texas 1835–1860* (Austin: The Texas State Historical Association, 1949).

Table 1

Regional Groupings Comparing Nativity vs. State of Residence
Prior to Living in Texas

Area	Nativity	Residence Prior to Texas	Loss or Gain
South	670	317	−353
Border South	1,204	1,453	+249
Border North	368	533	+165
North	95	41	−54
Foreign	40	33	−7

minimal moves based on childbirth data. Single, unattached adults and those without children were credited with but one migration, which in all probability grossly understates the case. Thus the Peters colonists performed in a manner compatible with the pattern of migration evidenced in other areas of American westward movement. They came primarily from the border South and border North and followed a flow pattern down to Missouri, into Arkansas, and finally to Texas. These moves were typical of the frontier "search" pattern.

The Peters colonists chose their land according to the "three w's": water, wood, and walnut trees. They settled east of the Balcones Fault, a geologic structure passing through the western edge of Fort Worth, in Tarrant County, and extending northward through the counties of Denton and Cooke.[8] To generalize broadly, the Balcones Fault marked a difference in soil, climate, and rainfall, literally separating the rancher from the farmer—

[8] *The Dallas Morning News, Texas Almanac 1961–62* (Dallas: A. H. Belo Corporation, 1961), p. 51.

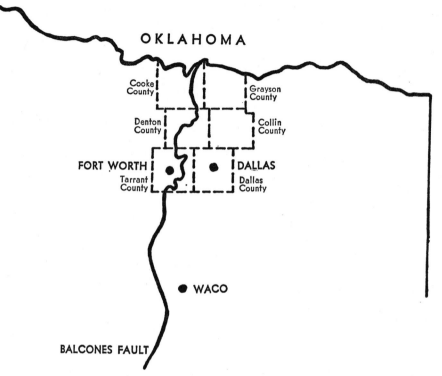

The Peters Colony and the Balcones Fault

and these colonists were farmers. The significance of the fault as related to land-selection patterns is shown in Table 2.

Eighty-one percent of the adults were farmers, and their preference for the lands east of the Balcones Fault is obvious. In general, they chose first the lowland drainage areas of the Trinity River and its tributaries, demonstrating a decided selectivity in terms of Dallas, Collin, and Grayson counties. Dallas County was their first choice, and, when that land was taken, they settled next in Collin and finally in Grayson counties.

Table 2

Land-Selection Patterns by Occupation

Occupation	Dallas	Collin	Grayson	Tarrant	Denton	Cooke	Total
Farmer	578	383	298	144	149	49	1601
Professional	24	28	18	6	3	0	79
Artisan	58	39	38	9	3	1	148
Laborer	20	0	90	0	0	0	110
Tradesman	13	7	10	2	1	0	33
County Employee	0	2	5	0	2	0	9
No Occupation	136	91	88	32	40	10	397
Total	829	550	547	193	198	60	2377

Why did these farmers, seeking good tillable land, at first pass over the excellent soil of Grayson and Collin? Their migration route took them west of Fort Smith, past Fort Towson in Indian Territory, and across the Red River in the neighborhood of Preston's Fort, where Mill Creek enters the Red River. Therefore, the first land in Texas to be appraised by these migrants was that of Grayson, then Collin, and finally Dallas County. The answer to this enigma has been recently settled through data available in the census of 1840, which was constructed from the available poll tax and local tax records.[9] These data show that 24.5 percent of the total land mass of Grayson County was already settled in 1840, before the Peters colonists arrived. These were the citizens of the Republic of Texas, many of whom claimed large land patents by virtue of their participation in the Texas war of independence. Collin had 11.9 percent of its land mass already claimed, but Dallas County was only 3.2 percent occupied.

[9] Gifford White, ed., *The 1840 Census of The Republic of Texas* (Austin: Pemberton Press, 1966).

It is apparent from these data that the land seeker, when he first entered Texas, moved into an area where a high percentage of the good farm land had already been claimed. The actual ratio of "good" land is, of course, considerably smaller than the land mass totals. In short, not all of the acreage in Grayson County was available for farming. As the settlers moved through Grayson into Collin, the scarcity of good land decreased, but the size of the existing spreads increased. Here were several farms in the six-thousand- and eight-thousand-acre category. No doubt the migrant by this time had heard of the available land in Dallas County, and, since he had the unrestricted right to choose his homesite anywhere in the six counties, he followed the rule of self-interest. The dominance of the eastern over the western counties is again evident when one considers the distribution of the heads of household: Dallas, Collin, and Grayson had 1,926 for 80 percent, while Tarrant, Denton, and Cooke had only 451 for 20 percent of the total.

Note must be made of the effects of extended families and their ties to the migration pattern. One family will serve as an excellent example—the Beemans from Illinois. One of them, James J. Beeman was with Colonel Denton and General Tarrant in the battle of Village Creek, just a few miles west of Arlington. The Beeman Papers consist of letters (1841–1846) from James J. Beeman and others to his family back in Illinois, and his memoirs written December 24, 1886.[10] One of his cousins, Margaret Beeman, became the first bride in Dallas when she married John

[10] "The Beeman Papers." Original letters (1841–1846) to relatives in Illinois plus Memoirs of James J. Beeman, written December 24, 1886. Now in the possession of a descendant, Professor William Beeman, mathematics department of The University of Texas at Arlington.

Neely Bryan, the founder of Dallas. Three Beeman brothers, John, James J., and Samuel, eventually brought a total of twenty-four children when they settled in Dallas County. John S. Beeman, the son of Samuel, wrote his family in 1841:

Father I think it is a great pity that you did not come this fall for you could have got 1 or 2 sections of land as for my part I expect 2 or three sections for coming to this country and if you and your boys over 17 years was here you could get a chance at land all that goes out in Trinity 2 or 3 sections, a single man one section or more. . . . p.s. James and David if you could come to Texas you could get land enough to do all and get paid for coming in the bargain. Bring with you your wives when you come for the more wives the more land. For my part I am going out on Trinity to get a Squaw and set her to raising cotton and dressing buffalo skins for me. J.S.B.[11]

In his memoirs, James J. Beeman refers to relatives near Paris, Texas, who provided employment during a period of economic stress. He also referred to the untimely death of Hamp Rattan, killed Christmas week of 1841 in the Trinity bottoms by the Indians. The two were related through Hamp's wife, Polly. She in turn was related to Dr. James Throckmorton of Collin County. In 1850, Polly was living near the doctor and Thomas Rattan; all three of them were from Illinois. By 1866, Dr. Throckmorton had forsaken the practice of medicine for politics and was governor of Texas. Beeman also refers to the Adam Haught family of Dallas County as being kin. Thus, in addition to the thirty-five immediate members of the Beeman family who came as the result of his letters, a considerable number of the extended family also migrated to Texas.

[11] Ibid.

Table 3

Marital Status by Counties

	1*	2	3	4	5	6	7	8
Dallas	339	333	63	37	10	3	40	4
Collin	215	252	42	14	1	3	17	6
Grayson	219	233	42	10	9	7	24	3
Subtotal	773	818	147	61	20	13	81	13
Tarrant	81	75	22	10	1	1	1	2
Denton	81	71	21	7	2	2	10	4
Cooke	19	27	9	0	0	0	5	0
Subtotal	181	173	52	17	3	3	16	6
Grand Total	954	991	199	78	23	16	97	19

* Marital Status Code

1. Single
2. Married
3. Widow or Widower
4. Married, but arrived in the colony single
5. Unmarried, but in charge of siblings
6. Married, no children of own, but with dependent children
7. Married, with children and dependent children
8. Widow, widower, with children and/or dependents

Table 4

Single Persons (Marriageable Ages) by Age and Sex

	Age																											
	18	19	20	21	22	23	24	25	26	27	28	29	30	31	32	33	34	35	36	37	38	39	40	41	42	43	44	45
M	80	59	74	74	55	47	27	43	24	18	7	8	19	11	8	4	2	9	7	0	3	2	8	1	1	3	2	4
F	53	31	21	19	20	10	4	12	2	5	2	2	2	1	1	0	2	2	0	0	0	2	0	0	0	0	0	2
Total	133	90	95	93	75	57	31	55	26	23	9	10	21	12	9	4	4	11	7	0	3	4	8	1	1	3	2	6

The recurring theme of "land for the boys" is illustrated in Table 3. By using subtle variations in the coding, it was possible to classify as separate groupings differing kinds of family arrangements. For example, some of these pioneers were married at the time of the census of 1850, but the land office records show that they were single when they first came to Texas, thus a special code for this type of family. Another code was used for surviving children who, when confronted with the trauma of loss of father and mother, chose to maintain the family as an entity.

A considerable amount of inherited information, some true and some legendary, exists about marriage and family customs in the pioneer period. Using the research data, it is possible to check these myths and to compare fact with fiction. The myths are (1) marriage at an early age and (2) the extreme marriageability of widows, particularly those with children. Almost every basic source book on the American family, whether in history, sociology, or economics, either states or assumes that people married at a tender age in colonial America and on the frontier.[12] The

[12] Adam Smith, *An Inquiry into the Nature and Cause of The Wealth of Nations* (New York: Random House, 1937), p. 71. Smith, the originator of this myth, puts it as follows, "The value of children is the greatest of all encouragements to marriage. We cannot, therefore, wonder that the people in North America should generally marry very young."

Clifford Kirkpatrick, *The Family as Process and Institution* (New York: Ronald Press Co., Second Edition, 1963), p. 121. ". . . marriage was regarded as desirable and early marriages were possible in a new rich country."

Ernest R. Groves, *The American Family* (Chicago-Philadelphia: J. B. Lippincott Company, 1934), p. 83. "Colonial conditions led to early marriage. Of Connecticut youth, for example, it was said by one writing in 1704, 'they generally marry very young, the males oftener, as I am told, under twenty years than above.' The girls often married at sixteen

total number of "single" people in this study was 1,159. However, this does not represent the true total of those "marriageable." The coding technique listed as single all males under age twenty-one if they had an occupation. In many instances, this system caused the listing of males as young as fourteen years of age. Obviously this age level did not include those of "marriageable" age.

Since 1837, by act of the Congress of the Republic of Texas, the age for marriage without the necessity of parental or court approval was twenty-one for the male and eighteen for the female.[13] Because this minimum differed greatly from the marriageable ages inherited from English Common Law (fourteen for the male and twelve for the female), it must be concluded that this Texas law represented a most progressive and advanced set of concepts. It must also be assumed that the Texas law reflected the cultural as well as the legal norms for this era. Therefore, for a true count of those eligible to marry, it is necessary to eliminate all persons under the legal age for marriage. Recognizing that there are both biological and social motives impelling most persons toward the altar, and that after one passes a certain age the drives are not quite so keen, those over age forty-five have been eliminated from the totals.

The data include those widows and widowers within the age

---

or younger, and an unmarried woman at twenty-five entered the ranks of the old maids."

Calhoun, *History of the American Family*, II, 11. "Conditions in the new American nation favored marriage, early marriage and high fecundity, and so long as pioneer conditions persisted, mating and breeding went on apace."

[13] H. P. N. Gammell, *The Laws of Texas* (Austin: Gammell Book Co., 1898), p. 1294.

range for it would appear that the loss of a mate, either by death or divorce, did not deter most persons from re-entering the married ranks. In fact, the first divorce granted in Dallas, in December of 1846, gave freedom to Charlotte Dalton from her husband, Joseph. That same afternoon she married Henderson Couch, the foreman of the jury that had granted the divorce that morning.[14] Frontier justice was apparently as quick in the divorce courts as at the end of a rope.

With these limitations in mind, arbitrary age limits for marriageable adults have been set at a minimum of eighteen for the female and twenty-one for the male and a maximum of forty-five. The adjusted totals yield 795 persons within the normal ages of marriage. These limits eliminated 144 males ranging from 15 through 20; 3 females under 18; and 35 persons over age 45. The data collated by ages and sex are shown in Table 4. A noticeable trend may be observed in these data. It would appear that the single ranks began to deplete soon after the females reached eighteen years of age. Since there was an average age difference of 5.97 years between husband and wife, this would explain the corresponding decrease of eligible males after age twenty-four.

These data pose an interesting enigma in that apparently something is anomalous in the total number for either the twenty-four– or the twenty-five–year-old grouping. Random chance could not explain the inordinately small number of the former nor the excess in the latter grouping. Unfortunately, vital statistics were not kept by the Bureau of the Census in those days (1825 and 1826), nor were records kept by their states of nativity (Arkansas, Missouri, Kentucky, Tennessee, Ohio, Indiana, and Illinois).

---

[14] John Henry Brown, *History of Dallas County, Texas* (Dallas: Milligan, Cornett & Farnham, Printers, 1887), p. 70.

One may conjecture that, for example, some kind of children's epidemic was prevalent around 1826 that decimated their ranks, or that some unusual historical event, such as the end of a war, brought on a surplus of births in 1825. Unfortunately, no evidence is available to solve this puzzle. One guess would be that the twenty-four–year (1826) grouping is too small, but this cannot be supported.

The ratio of male to female in this eligible single category is 3.2 to 1. A breakdown according to the number of males, females, and average age for each grouping and the ratio of the sexes by counties is shown in Table 5. This imbalance in favor of the single male is in keeping with the normal frontier settlement pattern. William Peterson, in his table "Migratory Selection of Types of Migration," described the pioneer movement as being characterized by an interest in the frontier lands, a dominance of young males, and a basis of individual motivation.[15]

Table 5

Single Persons (Marriageable Ages) by Sex, Average Age, Sex Ratio
by Counties

County	Single Males	Single Females	Male Dominance	Average Age—Male	Average Age— Female
Dallas	211	74	72.0%	23.9	22.5
Collin	141	43	76.6%	23.7	21.0
Grayson	131	44	74.8%	22.7	19.1
Tarrant	54	9	85.7%	23.1	19.7
Denton	49	21	70.0%	23.99	22.99
Cooke	13	3	81.3%	23.3	27.0

[15] William Peterson, *Population* (New York: Macmillan Co., 1961), p. 620.

One cannot help wondering as to what impact this sex ratio had in terms of the husband-wife relationships and within the family structure itself. As far as the female was concerned, hers need not have been a marriage motivated by economic necessity or propinquity. Quite obviously she did not have to "sell" herself into marriage to escape the degraded condition of singleness and the status of being an old maid. Further, she had a wide selection of eligible males from which she could choose and, since land ownership was a fixed variable, personality and other characteristics contributing to both compatibility and a shared partnership type of marriage might well have been the free variable. These facts may have been significant in establishing the basis for the trend away from the traditional patriarchal relationship.

It is all too apparent that the female should have been at a premium, yet neither the attractions of marital bliss nor the blandishments of the "eager" male were strong enough to induce many of them to tie the knot. Perhaps there were overpowering reasons for the apparent delay beyond the legal age for marriage. Could it also have been true that a significant portion of the males were interested or involved in other matters that had precedence at this period of their lives?

In summary, there were 1,182 married couples in the Peters Colony, a total of 2,364 married persons. This represented only 28 percent of the population. Just as in the population of the United States today (at least half are below the age of twenty-six) the Peters colonists were also "youth oriented." They had a work force of 2,377 persons, not including wives, but if they are added, the total is 3,559 persons in the available work force. Subtracting those not legally eligible to marry, the total is 3,412 persons within the marriageable age grouping. Using this as a base it appears that 70 percent of those eligible to marry were married at the time of the census. There were sixty-four single persons over age twenty-six still not married; they represented 1.3 percent of the total adult population. Thus, of the 30 percent not married but of marriageable age, 28.7 percent would eventually marry but were single as of 1850.

The data collected also showed those couples who were single when they arrived in the colony but who had married before the census of 1850. An analysis of the seventy-eight newlyweds is most revealing. Certain traits and values that were operative on the American frontier were those apparently common to other societies. A man might have to postpone the time of his marriage, but when he was ready to marry he chose a mate from an age grouping noted for its youth, vigor, and cooperativeness. He totally ignored his own age group, unless he happened to be young.

Nine of the females were under the legal age for marriage yet were married. Sixty-four of the females were twenty-three years of age or under at the time of the census. Unfortunately, the time or date of the marriage is not known, but we may assume that there was a direct relationship between the number of children in the family and the number of years the couple had been married. The circumstances at this period of our national development placed a premium on having children, and these people did have the solid economic base of free land. Both of these factors point to a correlation between the number of years of marriage and the number of children.

Interesting data reflecting age at marriage would therefore be found for the childless couples on the assumption that they had not been married long enough to have their first-born. For the Peters Colony, this grouping numbered twenty-four couples and is shown in Table 6, spaced by matching ages of husband and wife according to the counties of residence. Other than the fact that eight of the females were under the legal age for marriage (but not close to the English Common Law minimum), it is apparent that the males were far from youthful at marriage. When it is remembered that each of these males had the secure base of free land on which to build a marriage, their ages even more significantly deny the early-age myth.

The second of the myths concerning marriage customs on the frontier was the extreme marriageability of the widow, particularly the widow with children. As proposed by Adam Smith, this myth is founded on the economic necessity for hands to work the

Table 6

Single, Childless Colonists Who Married After Arrival
by Age and County

Dallas		Collin		Grayson		Tarrant		Denton	
M	F	M	F	M	F	M	F	M	F
23	17	25	16	25	16	23	16	23	16
22	18	31	16	27	17	19	18	33	19
29	19	38	20	23	17	26	20	24	20
27	19			20	18	25	26		
22	20			27	23	38	29		
27	20								
30	20								
24	26								

land.[16] In the study area, the attractiveness of the widow was further enhanced because, as a Peters colonist, she possessed land —free land. Connor, who also deals with this "legend," limits his comments to the Peters group, while this study encompasses the total census.[17]

In the Peters Colony, a total of 174 women were the head of their family group. Of this number 49 were "single" and residing in another person's home. This group probably included the hired help or girl servants of one type or another. Of this grouping, 21 were related to Peters colonists; in other words they were children of the colonists who were gainfully employed outside the home.

The matter of occupation for women in 1850, as far as the census is concerned, was a commentary on the status of women, all women, at this time. They may have been sexual and economic necessities, but they were not yet to be dignified with the status of an occupation. That column of the census sheet was scrupulously left blank in all but three instances. The first two involved Dallas County schoolteachers, Elizabeth Baker and Mrs. J. W. Latimer. The third case provided one of the brighter moments in what is otherwise a dreary exercise in research. Somehow one can visualize the moral judgment of the census taker in Ellis County when he called at this "lady's" home. She had three children, each with a different surname, none of which matched her own. She had practiced her profession, or spread her affection, as the case may be, from Michigan to Arkansas, and finally in Texas. Since she was a woman, customary census practice re-

[16] Smith, *Wealth of Nations*, p. 71.
[17] Connor, *Peters Colony*, pp. 104–105.

quired that the blank for occupation be left empty. The temptation, however, was too great, and the census taker could not resist the urge to put down "lone grass widow."

The remaining "single" persons constituted the widows of the colony and numbered 125 in all. They had a total of 305 children still residing in the home for an average of 2.55 children per adult. Using the state of birth of the mother and comparing that with the state of nativity of the children gives a total of 246 known migrations—about 2 migrations per family. Seventy-eight of these women were Peters colonists and claimants of free land, while forty-seven were not. At the time of the census, sixty-five of the widows were without land, and, in the case of the Peters colonists, this meant that economic survival necessitated selling their headrights. The landless group ranged in age from eighteen to ninety-nine years with an average age of fifty-one. Since this is a relatively old group, they had an average of only 1.66 children still in the home. In other words, by the time a mother had reached this age, most of her children would have married and left the home.

The sixty widows with land present an entirely different picture, and one wonders, with Connor, why they had not remarried. Their ages ranged from 21 to 64 with an average of 42.6. Forty-seven of the sixty were Peters colonists. They owned land ranging from 50 to 18,700 acres. The average number of acres owned was 994 and the average number of children still in the home was 3.5. Taking the data related to the two myths, the unmarried adults with their 3.2-to-1 male ratio, and comparing it with the data on the landed widows, we can only conclude that Adam Smith's hypothesis did not work, at least not in this part of the frontier.

One fact stands out with regard to the head of household in 1850: it is that the urge to move out to the frontier was during his "prime of life" period. Almost three-fifths of the heads of household were within the 20–39 age grouping, while just a fraction over 12 percent were over fifty years of age. The data in Table 7 support that reported by Merle Curti in his studies of Wisconsin for 1850, 1860, 1870, and 1880.[18] The differences are due to the fact that his collations are in terms of "All Gainfully Employed," while these data are arranged in terms of "Head of Household."

The family was probably the first, if not the basic, institution to evolve to meet fundamental human needs. Conclusive evidence indicates that on the frontier the ties of family were indeed strong and lasting. The family in crisis presented an opportunity to muster support of a tangible nature to preserve it and the family name as well. The data in Table 8 include the children of broken families, still maintaining the family form, but under the leadership of one of the older children. As an indication of community support, instances were found where the neighbors stepped in to help the survivors when they could not master the situation alone. Here is found the frontier version of Aid to Dependent Children, and it would appear that the settlers cared for their own better than do we of the twentieth century. The limits of contemporary responsibility often do not extend beyond the nuclear family circle and seldom reach beyond our own bloodlines. Table 8 could be considered nothing more or less than statistical data. It also represents, however, the heights to which a human can reach

[18] Merle Curti, *The Making of An American Community* (Stanford: Stanford University Press, 1959), p. 56.

Table 7

Age Distribution of Heads of Household
by Counties

Age	Dallas	Collin	Grayson	Tarrant	Denton	Cooke
10–19	16.3	13.9	17.6	18.0	13.1	8.3
20–29	36.0	36.4	34.4	33.7	36.4	44.9
30–39	22.5	23.0	20.7	21.4	23.2	16.7
40–49	12.1	13.9	13.0	16.1	16.2	16.7
50–59	8.7	8.9	9.9	9.8	7.1	11.7
60–69	2.1	2.2	3.7	0.5	3.0	1.7
70–79	2.1	1.3	0.5	0.5	1.0	0.0
80–89	0.2	0.4	0.0	0.0	0.0	0.0
90–99	0.0	0.0	0.2	0.0	0.0	0.0

Table 8

Orphaned Children Caring for Brothers and Sisters

Age	14	16	16	16	17	17	18	19	19	19	19	20	21	21	21	24	24	25	30	30	30	35	36	36
M		x	x	x	x		x	x	x	x	x	x		x	x	x	x		x	x		x	x	x
F	x					x							x					x			x			
Brothers & Sisters	3	2	3	1	6	3	2	1	2	2	5	2	1	3	2	1	2	1	8	2	2	4	1	1

when confronted with the dissolution of the family. The immediate impression is hard to reject: seventeen of the twenty-three persons were male, yet they assumed the responsibility of rearing their brothers and sisters.

When the circumstances were too difficult to surmount, the neighbors assisted the survivors. For example, the Jeremiah Holford (Halford?) family of Collin County had taken in Sarah Scott, fourteen years old. In the next house down the road lived the family of John Hill who had taken in Amiza Scott, a twelve-year-old boy, and Isabell Scott, eight years old. Two houses farther down the road was the Isaac Edwards family, which had employed Joseph Scott, a seventeen-year-old farmer. The Scotts, thanks to the help of the neighbors, had lost neither their individual identity nor their family name.

It is increasingly apparent that there was a compulsion paramount to whatever urges there might have been to marry early, as the myth consistently insists. That compelling necessity was the close tie of family, and the need was for total cooperation on the part of all of the family in order to survive. More than mere survival was the realization on the part of all concerned that real security could, under these conditions, be achieved.

Dr. and Mrs. John Cole arrived in Dallas County from Arkansas in 1843. With them they brought their three younger sons. Their older married children had left the home. At the time of the census of 1850, Polly was a widow, but her sons, ages 20, 23, and 27, still lived at home and were unmarried. Polly was born in Virginia, her youngest son in Arkansas, and the other two in Tennessee. This is a typical example of the migration path. By 1850, Polly Cole, who had 18,700 acres, was the largest landowner in Dallas County. In the entire Peters Colony she was exceeded as a landowner only by M. T. Johnson of Tarrant County, who had 25,000 acres. Each of the sons, still single and living at home, eventually married, so the fact that they did not marry until relatively late was not caused by a lack of interest or eligibility. Had wealth alone been the deciding factor, any one of these young men would have been a prize catch for an unmarried lass in Dallas County. The point is that they were not yet ready to cut the ties of family, and they were needed to continue the economic struggle for family security. In fact, they have their modern counterpart in the industrialist who does not know when to stop his continuous struggle for success. Both the Coles and the contemporary tycoon might have been victims of the puritanical compulsion to work. However, the nineteenth-century puritan had a different orientation—the compelling ties of family. The need for total and united effort heightened the ingroup feeling, and under frontier conditions it was the direct result of the demands for survival in order to conquer the hazards of the primitive conditions.

Another factor tending to substantiate the point of economic cooperation is the fact that the families of Dallas and Collin counties had the largest percentage of children old enough to be in the available work force. Being older, and thus available to work the land, they tipped the economic balance scales. Dallas and Collin counties were also the leaders in terms of population and land ownership.

We now sum up some of the major demographic characteristics of the pioneer family in the north central Texas area circa 1850: There was a total of 7,710 white, nonmilitary colonists in the six-county area, including 1,182 married couples with a total of 4,563 children still residing in the home. The average age for the husband was 37.53 and that of his wife 31.56. This produced an age difference between the husband and wife of 5.97 years. They had an average of 3.86 children still residing in the home. There was a significant number of unmarried adults with a sex ratio of 3.2 to 1 in favor of the males. Furthermore, there was a large number of widows, 125 to be exact, who could be divided into two significantly different groupings—those with and those without land. Those with land were younger, owned fair-sized land holdings, and were predominantly Peters colonists. The majority of the heads of household were in the "prime of life" category of 20–39 years of age.

The evidence would further indicate that "marriage at an early age" was a myth not supportable by the data. In fact, the findings of this study would support the statistics on "age at first marriage" reported by the Bureau of the Census.[19] This report shows that in 1890 the average age for the male was 26.1 and the female 22.0, and for each ten years of the census since then the figure has declined. The facts reported in this study would fit ideally into a backward projection of ages. Thus, if there is a "marriage at an early age" problem it is peculiarly a twentieth-century phenomenon. The evidence also refutes the myth first promulgated by Adam Smith concerning the marriageability of widows. Further studies involving other areas of frontier settlement must be made before Smith's myth can be categorically refuted, but the Peters Colony data very definitely raise the question of its validity.

Substantial evidence in the data suggests that the frontier family was culture bound with strong sentimental ties and values.

[19] Henry Bowman, *Marriage For Moderns*, Fifth Edition (New York: McGraw-Hill, 1965), p. 313.

The data revealed that, even when faced with the death of both parents, the remnants of the family continued to cling together in a modified form. One surviving "family" was headed by a fourteen-year-old girl, who was caring for three of her brothers and sisters. Thus, data from the Peters Colony suggest that the family unit was the unifying force on the American frontier.

THE MUZZLE-LOADING RIFLE

Frontier Tool

〜〜〜〜〜〜〜〜〜〜〜〜〜〜〜〜〜〜〜〜〜〜〜〜〜〜〜〜〜〜〜

BY ROBERT L. WILLIAMSON

THE MUZZLE-LOADING RIFLE was many things. It was a work of art—technologically perceptive, keenly designed, esthetically pleasing. It was food, clothing, amusement, companionship. It was money in the pocket. A man carried it, slept alongside it, decorated it, taught his son to use it. One thing it was not—a good military weapon. The fact that it is usually remembered as such clouds its significance on the frontier.

Its claim to American credentials is impeccable: it immigrated from Europe. In the New World it gave in to new demands, changed its form without losing its identity. Pennsylvania craftsmen in crude shops lengthened its grooved barrel to increase its accuracy and to insure total burning of its black powder charge. Its bore was reduced to save expensive lead and powder. Its flintlock and trigger guard were made rugged. Its stock was curved and lengthened; sight and balance were improved. Pride in manufacture and ownership were expressed on stock and barrel, in graceful scrolls and inlays—artistry not commonly wasted on military arms. Before the 1730's a distinctly American rifle had evolved, clearly adapted to frontier conditions, used most effectively by the frontier rifleman. The rifleman was never, in essence, a soldier.

Never a soldier, he occasionally went to war. His rifle accompanied him, as did his hunting shirt, his moccasins, his leggings, his neighbors. He was a good scout, could become an effective guerrilla, could harass and raid. In a fight between armies, he gave way to infantrymen with their muskets. Accuracy and range were overwhelmed by speed, group firepower, and bayonets. The soldier could load his musket three times while the rifleman loaded once. Skill in marksmanship was not a necessity for massed infantry closing with a foe; a clubbed rifle was poor competition for a bayonet. American rifles were not generally adapted to receive bayonets—a military necessity—until breech-loading and repeating arms became common, until the individual rifleman acquired firepower. To repeat, the muzzle-loading rifle was not basically a military weapon.

The most romantic mythology of the rifleman as an invincible fighter has grown up around his encounters with Indians. He fought them, when he was forced to, at a disadvantage. One frontiersman put it this way: "An Indian could discharge a dozen arrows while a man was loading a gun, and if they could manage to draw our fire all at once they had us at their mercy unless we had a safe retreat."[1]

As soon as a man fired his rifle, he was unarmed for thirty seconds to a minute, longer if he gave in to nerves. Group tac-

[1] Noah Smithwick, *The Evolution of a State or Recollections of Old Texas Days* (Austin, Texas: Gammel Book Co., 1900), p. 221.

tics, timed firing, threat instead of action, slow retreat—these
were the rifleman's main hope for survival in war. Once the
frontier passed onto prairies and plains, into the horse-Indian
culture, the weakness of the rifle as a weapon became critical. It
was never designed for use on horseback, or against horsemen
who insisted on closing. Western gunsmiths adapted it to new
conditions as best they could. They made it lighter, shortened its
barrel and stock, created a Plains model. It was *carried* on horseback but rarely *used* on horseback. It was still too slow and difficult to load, still not suited to head-on, eyeball-to-eyeball combat.
Still not a good military weapon.

If the frontiersman's main business had been fighting, he
would have been forced to develop a better weapon, to invade
the wilderness in larger parties, to assume a slower pace, and the
muzzle-loading rifle would not have had the same significance on
the frontier. The rifle was married to the frontier for more than a
century because it was vital to daily living, not because it was
useful in interludes of organized warfare or occasional Indian
encounters. That secondary utility was merely a welcome bonus
to its owner. Its true significance was that of a common, adaptable
tool. By definition, a tool is "an instrument or apparatus necessary to a person in the practice of his vocation or profession."[2]
The vocation, the profession of the frontiersman was to make living bearable, while a virgin, sometimes harsh, environment was
changed into comfortable civilization. The rifle was his chief
support.

Imagine a man with an urge for land, adventure, escape, satis-

[2] *Webster's Third New International Dictionary of the English Language, Unabridged* (Springfield, Mass.: G. & C. Merriam Co., 1963).

faction of curiosity. Just beyond him is country to satisfy it if he has the skills and the determination to hold on. He leaves the settlements, aiming west. Until he returns, or the settlements overtake him, he is in contest with the land itself. Potentially, the rewards are glittering; he must last out time to collect them.

The waiting was the critical time for the man who intended to stay, who brought his family with him or built it on the spot. There could be no food, no money crop immediately, no easy restocking of supplies. When a man chose a place to stop—with or without a family—his immediate necessity was for shelter and food. He must seek them out, even as he prepared for the future. There was no escape from the present. Clothes wore out, hunger came, money ran short. Nothing waited for land to be cleared, worked, and planted. Those tasks accomplished, returns were still months away. Surpluses and their profits might be years ahead. For several years, most of a man's living, much of his money must come from the wild land around him. Markets were at a distance; transportation was difficult to or from them. Only the most valuable goods, not necessarily the most expensive, were carried either way. Shelter, clothing, food, and furniture must be produced locally, from whatever resources the country provided. Cash to buy necessities the land did not furnish—lead, powder, salt, tools, a few staples—must come from goods simple to preserve, simple to transport under primitive conditions. Hunting and its variants—trapping, trading with the Indians—furnished workable solutions to many economic problems as a frontier was gradually consumed by civilization. Hunters, trappers, traders, explorers, travelers—those who lived on a frontier without attempting to settle it permanently—faced basically the same problems as those who came to stay. They used the same tools and techniques for living as did the permanent settlers, their followers.

The most pressing and continuing need was food. Frontier people were meat eaters. As a Kentucky tavern keeper put it in 1807, ". . . even the children were fed on game . . ."[3] Writing of another frontier, twenty years later and hundreds of miles westward, a Texas blacksmith elaborated the constant theme. "Game was the sole dependence of many families and I fixed up many an old gun that I wouldn't have picked up in the road, knowing that it was all that stood between a family and the gaunt wolf at the door, as well as the Indians."[4]

The muzzle-loading rifle was a tool designed for harvesting game. It had no equal for more than a hundred years. It was simple to maintain and operate. It was dependably accurate at ranges up to a hundred yards. In the hands of an expert, it was dangerous to a man-sized target within two hundred yards. When luck joined skill, it killed at much greater distances. To a man who could put his first shot where he wanted it, slowness in loading was not a great disadvantage in hunting. Hunting was a chore usually reserved for men and boys along the frontier. Occasionally a woman, through force of circumstances, showed the way.

[3] Reuben Gold Thwaites, ed., *Early Western Travels 1748–1846: A Series of Annotated Reprints of Some of the Best and Rarest Contemporary Volumes of Travel, Descriptive of the Aborigines and Social and Economic Conditions in the Middle and Far West, During the Period of Early American Settlement*, 32 vols. (Cleveland, Ohio: Arthur H. Clark Co., 1904), IV, *Cuming's Tour to the Western Country (1807–1809)*, 177.

[4] Smithwick, *Evolution of a State*, p. 18.

A Texas traveler of the 1830's tells of a matron who must have studied carefully on the care and feeding of husbands. Her husband took his ease, engaged in conversation. She took her rifle and sauntered after game, successfully. She killed as many as eighty deer in one season. She supported her family.[5]

Frontier records are filled with references that underline the extent to which families depended upon game for food. The dependence continued even after a region had been settled for several years, after it had begun to show some of the trappings of civilization—a makeshift school, a crossroads cluster of tavern and cabins. David Meriwether tells a typical tale. In his lifetime he followed the frontier from the Ohio River to New Mexico Territory. In 1805 he lived with his family on a frontier farm near Louisville, Kentucky. He writes that before Christmas that year they had filled their meat house—in Texas that would be called a smokehouse—with game. Row upon row of deer hams and saddles, lines of raccoons and "possums," the whole topped off with forty-five turkeys. Everything was salted and prepared for smoking.[6]

In 1802 a French official came to the United States to study forests and agriculture in frontier areas. He described the settlers in the southern reaches of the Alleghenies as excellent hunters. In the autumn they invaded the woods for bear. Bear meat was a major part of their diet in the fall of the year. Then the animals were likely to be fat and sluggish—easy prey to riflemen. The

[5] Mary Austin Holley, *Texas* (Lexington, Kentucky: J. Clarke & Co., 1836), pp. 135–136.

[6] Robert A. Griffen, ed., *David Meriwether: My Life in the Mountains and on the Plains: The Newly Discovered Autobiography* (Norman: University of Oklahoma Press, 1965), pp. xv, 10–11.

frontiersmen of the region praised bear meat above all other, saying a man could eat immense quantities of it with no ill effects.[7] A generation later, their heirs on the Plains would say the same thing about buffalo meat and demonstrate their faith to all doubters. The bears provided, in addition to hams, oil or grease for various home uses—cooking, oiling guns, fueling lamps, greasing equipment, and grooming a man's hair. The skins not used at home for bedding, rugs, and robes could be packed to market for sale. A good skin brought a dollar and a half or two dollars on the market at that time. More than enough to repay time, effort, powder, and lead spent getting it there.

A few years later, a sight-seeing Englishman told a better tale. He met a young hunter near the falls of the Ohio River and engaged him in conversation about the country. The hunter said he and a partner had killed 135 bears in only six weeks' time. Hides in good condition were then bringing six to ten dollars each.[8] Making generous allowance for optimistic accounting, this still leaves a tidy sum to supplement a frontiersman's yearly income. Hunting was more than mere fun.

Group migrations onto the frontier were not uncommon in certain regions. In Texas, during the 1830's and 1840's, several German settlements began as group projects. Many of the settlers came directly from Germany, unprepared for the frontier experience. The young people among them—and later the second generation—would adapt to the new environment with a minimum of trouble. For the first few years, however, such set-

[7] Thwaites, *Early Western Travels, III, André Michaux's Travels into Kentucky, 1793–1796. Francois André Michaux's Travels West of Alleghany Mountains, 1802; Thaddeus Mason Harris's Journal of a Tour Northwest of Alleghany Mountains, 1803,* 289.
[8] Thwaites, *Early Western Travels,* IV, 137.

tlers were likely to suffer hunger and other hardships arising from
their lack of skill in frontier craft. For awhile, they would de-
pend upon others to supply their needs.

A German scientist stopping in Fredericksburg in 1847 has
described a trading session between the townspeople and a party
of Shawnees.[9] The Indians entered town with a drove of pack
horses and set up business in front of the Verein Building. Their
stock was principally bear meat and oil. The oil was carried in
deer skins, cased and stripped from the carcasses in the manner
used by the herdsman before the time of Abraham. The hair was
scraped away, the openings laced with rawhide, the seams
smeared with tallow—a wilderness keg constructed. Riflemen
from the Alleghenies to the Rockies made such containers for
countless uses. The Indians of this party traded individually,
some having as much as sixty gallons of bear oil to dispose of, at
a dollar per gallon in goods or money. Settlers came from every
direction to get the oil. It was the most popular cooking fat in
town, doubling as the chief illuminant. The average frontiersman, however, gathered it for himself.

Hunting was so necessary a part of living along the frontier
that it was studied and practiced almost as a skilled trade. The
masters laughed at the clumsy attempts of the apprentices, then
helped them with the mysteries. Accounts by settlers make no
more of hunting skill than of kindred talents—the ability to
plow, to use an axe, to whittle out the uprights and crosspieces
for a chair. All are taken as a matter of course. It is only because
of the numerous passing references to them that their vital im-

---

[9] Ferdinand Roemer, *Texas with Particular Reference to German
Immigration and the Physical Appearance of the Country*, trans. Oswald
Mueller (San Antonio, Texas: Standard Printing Co., 1935), p. 232.

portance in daily affairs becomes apparent. The visitor on the frontier—the merchant accompanying his goods, the circuit rider on his rounds, the author seeking material, the adventurer—was more impressed with special skills. He noted and exclaimed over them, especially the use of the rifle. Gustave Dresel, traveling along the Texas frontier in 1839, wondered at the skill of children.[10] He was staying with a family in Montgomery County. With the politeness of a guest, he referred to their holding as a plantation. It was not such in the sense that four or five generations of romantic Southerners have manufactured for the term. It was a backwoods farm, a family operation. As a routine practice, surprising to no one except Dresel, the twelve-year-old son of the family took his rifle one morning and walked into the woods, after a deer or turkey. He worked his way into a thicket —southeast Texas abounds with them even today—and came face to face with a big cat. Dresel calls it a "leopard." "Leopard" crops up frequently in Texas frontier accounts, applied locally to different members of the cat family. It might mean a jaguar, a spotted cat, a wildcat, even a panther. In this case, it was probably a panther. The boy snapped a shot, seriously wounding the animal. As it reared and threshed about in the brush, he calmly reloaded his rifle. His second shot dropped the cat as it charged him. He then blazed a trail from the thicket and returned home for help. There was a valuable pelt to be taken. He had earned praise. He was learning the way.

If it was indeed a panther the youth killed, he did more than secure a good hide. These cats were a destructive raucous nui-

---

[10] Max Freund, ed. and trans., *Gustav Dresel's Houston Journal: Adventures in North America and Texas, 1837–1841* (Austin: University of Texas Press, 1954), p. 82.

sance to the backwoods settler. They were demons among hogs and calves. The suspected presence of a panther about the place was enough to send the men and dogs out, day or night. The persistent attention of a panther to a family's livestock was sufficient excuse to call in the neighbors on a joint eradication project.

As a young man, Daniel Shipman lived with his family on a farm in Stephen F. Austin's Texas colony. After supper one night in 1826, the family was sitting quietly in the cabin. By the light of a dry-cane torch, one member was reading aloud to the others. Suddenly, they heard a pig launch a squeal—cut off in mid-breath. The father grabbed a torch. The boys caught up their rifles. Outside, they discovered a panther, mouthing a half-grown hog. Daniel fired offhand, wounding the cat. The panther dropped the hog, ran toward a bayou. The boys set their dogs on him and ran after the pack. The hounds brought the animal to bay on a footlog over the bayou, holding him there for the hunters. By the light of a torch held behind him, Daniel shot a second time. The panther fell into the water, dead. Later the boys fished him out for his hide.[11]

The war against panthers was not confined to the Texas frontier. John James Audubon, in the first quarter of the nineteenth century, rambled the back country frontier in his search for American birds. He stopped often with settlers in remote cabins, lived with them for weeks at a time. He was as keen an observer of humans as of birds. He recorded what he saw of frontier living with incisive understanding. On one occasion he spent some time with a settler who was trying to carve out a farm near the Cold

[11] Daniel Shipman, *Frontier Life: 58 Years in Texas*, Reprint of original 1879 edition (Pasadena, Texas: Abbotsford Publishing Co., 1965), pp. 57–58.

Water River in Mississippi. The man was plagued with a "painter." It took a tithe of his pigs, relished his calves for variety, and insulted his dignity. Occasionally, it made off with a carcass he had hung for his own larder. Audubon offered to help destroy the animal. The host thanked him, then went in search of reinforcements. This was the way of the frontier.

He notified his neighbors for several miles around that he was going after the panther. On the chosen day, Audubon, the farmer, his sons, and five neighbors set out on horseback, rifles in hand, dogs around them in an eager pack. Later, they cut the trail; the chase began. After a run of some time, the hounds bayed—treed the cat. The hunters rode to the sound. One rider fired, wounding the animal; the chase was on again. When the horses became winded, the men dismounted. They hobbled the horses, removed the saddles and bridles, followed the dogs on foot. Just before sundown the pack treed again. The riflemen came up; three fired at once, knocking the panther down among the dogs. Afraid the dogs might be injured, the host stepped into the melee, placed his rifle against the cat's body, fired point blank to end the scramble. The hunters took the pelt, leaving the carcass to the dogs. The sons, paying the penalty of youth, were sent a long walk home to do the chores. The men spent the night on the spot, shot a deer for their supper, and washed it down with whiskey carried for such emergencies. The following morning they hunted up their horses and returned home, a routine task finished.[12]

Panther, bear, deer, buffalo, whatever the game might be, the inexperienced hunter's greatest difficulty was with himself. Al-

<hr>

[12] John James Audubon, *Delineations of American Scenery and Character* (New York: G. A. Baker & Co., 1926), pp. 43–47.

though fearless, a dead shot, and in desperate need, when he faced important game something happened to his nerves. Deer might surround him in droves, in perfect safety. One young hunter records that he shot away "pounds of lead" in such a situation and got laughed at for his troubles.[13] With attention to the advice of experts, with practice, the beginner could improve. He must, if he stayed on the frontier.

A beginner's first important kill was likely to be an occasion for celebration, his admission to the clan. Young Noah Smithwick lived for a time with a family in Josiah Bell's Texas settlement. Game supplied a major part of their food. Smithwick went out with the men and boys to hunt—a frequent chore. Countless times he failed to kill his deer. Finally, on a lone hunt, he succeeded. The boys saw him returning across the prairie, carcass on his back. They called out the entire family to meet him, hoisted him to their shoulders, carried him triumphantly to the house.[14] He was initiated, entitled to the respect due a provider.

Another young hunter records a more lively ceremony. W. A. A. Wallace joined a surveying expedition on the Texas frontier in 1837. A day out from the settlements, the group set up a temporary camp. Wallace walked out to try his hand at hunting. In the frontier manner, the party lived off the country. As a boy in Virginia, Wallace had shot small game; this was his first attempt at deer. With uncommon luck for a beginner, he soon killed one. Back in camp, he tried nonchalance. The men suspected it was his first deer, grilled him relentlessly. Finally, he confessed the charge. Immediately, several of them grabbed him, wrestled him down, held him. The others smeared him liberally

[13] Smithwick, *Evolution of a State*, p. 29.
[14] Ibid.

with the animal's blood, thereby inducting him into the brother-
hood of hunters.[15]

In a society where the rifle was so much a part of daily life,
techniques for its use were discussed, demonstrated, and sometimes passed on in written form. Rufus B. Sage traveled frontier
trails from Texas to the Rocky Mountains; along the way he
recorded helpful hints for turkey hunters.[16] Sage went after the
birds at night, by moonlight. He advised the hunter to lie in wait
at a roost until the moon was high. At that time he should stand
so that a bird was between him and the moon, the turkey's
shadow on the hunter's face. He should raise his rifle slowly,
fire at the precise moment the front sight entered the shadow.
He was almost certain to make a center shot. Dozens might be
killed before the flock was aroused enough to fly. Sage always
tells a good story, and his interest in methods is typical of the
frontier rifleman. Meat was his object. He wanted to know the
easiest and surest way to get it.

Night hunting was common along the frontier. Days were
filled with myriad never-finished tasks. In 1811 Henry Brackenridge left a law practice in St. Louis to join a party of trappers
headed up the Missouri River.[17] Several miles above St. Charles,
the party camped for the night on a sand bar. Brackenridge was

[15]John C. Duval, *The Adventures of Big Foot Wallace the Texas
Ranger and Hunter*, 4th ed. (Macon, Georgia: Remsen & Haffelfinger,
1870), p. 5.

[16]Rufus B. Sage, *Rocky Mountain Life or Startling Scenes and Peri-
lous Adventures in the Far West*, Star Library (Dayton, Ohio: Edward
Canby, n.d.), p. 223.

[17]Thwaites, *Early Western Travels*, VI, *Brackenridge's Journal up
the Missouri, 1811; Franchère's Voyage to Northwest Coast, 1811–
1814*, 35.

puzzled by a scaffold located near the river's edge. He learned that settlers in the area climbed the scaffold at night to shoot deer by moonlight, when the animals came out of nearby thickets to escape mosquitos. The stand was a slaughterhouse for an entire community of frontier farmers gathering food.

Night hunting techniques varied. Fire-hunting was a favorite practice in every back country region. William Bollaert traveled the Texas frontier in 1842. He was unexpectedly, almost fatally, introduced to the art of fire-hunting. He and a friend left Houston to ride to a settlement near the Trinity River. Night caught them on the prairie. Riding on after dark, they saw a light ahead of them and supposed it was a house. As they approached, a ball hummed past their horses; they heard the crack of a rifle. Their yells brought up a party of hunters. The light came from a fire pan used to shine the eyes of deer. This time it worked on horses.[18]

Settlers after meat or hides used several variations of fire-hunting. There must be enough light to show the front sight of the rifle, to reflect from an animal's eyes up to a hundred yards away. One method was to build a small fire in a pan or pot. The container must have a bail, a handle. "Light pine" was often used for fuel. This was gathered in the form of pine knots and pieces of heart wood from a fallen tree. Such wood has a high pitch content and burns fiercely, even in damp weather. A lone hunter had to carry the fire for himself. He could run an iron rod, a poker, or a freshly cut green stick through the handle and carry it over his shoulder—left shoulder for a right-handed man. By moving the stick about, he could direct the glow from the fire.

[18] William Eugene Hollon and Ruth Lapham Butler, eds., *William Bollaert's Texas* (Norman: University of Oklahoma Press, 1956), p. 112.

When he shined a pair of eyes, he tried to move in to a range
of forty or fifty yards. With his left hand he could maneuver the
stick into position to form a rest for his rifle. Results depended
upon the skill and experience of the shooter. A long-handled
warming pan, if such were available, could be used to carry the
fire. Obviously, several men working together had an easier time
of it.[19] Some hunters dispensed with a fire pan and carried a
torch. A pine knot, a bundle of dry cane, an oil-soaked rag fixed
to a handle—almost anything would serve. It was reported in the
1840's that some Texas hunters had hit on the idea of fixing
candles and reflectors to the fronts of their hats.[20] Half a century
later, rural rabbit hunters would sport carbide lamps. A new generation depends on battery powered lights.

Not all fire-hunting occurred at night. In 1825 Sylvester Pattie
and his son James took a trapping party to the Gila River in New
Mexico. Typically, they depended upon rifles to supply their
food. On one occasion, James and a friend left camp to search
for strayed horses. They spotted a cave in the rocks and turned
aside to inspect it. Signs indicated that a bear had denned up inside. Pattie was eager to go in after the animal. His companion
preferred to wait outside. The boys gathered pine knots; James
fashioned a torch. He lashed it to a stick, held it along his rifle
barrel to light the sight, and entered the cave. About twenty yards
from the entrance, he found his bear—he fired as it reared over
him. In his excitement, Pattie fell and lost his rifle. The torch
went out; James scrambled outside. With another torch, and his
friend's rifle, he re-entered the cave, found the bear dead. The

19 Ibid., p. 277.
20 Ibid., p. 112, n. 31.

animal was skinned, its carcass butchered and dried for future use. The fat produced ten gallons of oil. A profitable adventure.[21]

There is no way to determine accurately the number of animals that one man, or one family, might kill and use in a single year. Contemporary records leave no doubt that the number was large. An Ohio traveler in 1807 stopped for the night at a cabin below Marietta. His host told him that a man could kill as many as two hundred deer and eighty bears in one season in that area.[22] The same traveler says that the settlers west of the Alleghenies depended more on hunting than on farming for their subsistence.[23] An Illinois resident of the 1820's writes that eight men in his neighborhood killed about three hundred squirrels between dawn of one day and noon of the next.[24] A Texan living on a farm near the Red River in 1822 says that his family lived mainly by hunting. He often took as many as six deer hides in a day, worth twenty cents a pound at market.[25] A European observer noted in 1832 that one young man regularly supplied New Harmony, Indiana, residents with wild turkeys, at twenty-five cents per bird. He frequently had ten or fifteen hanging on his horse at one time.[26] A Texas traveler along the Brazos River in 1837 says the

[21] Thwaites, *Early Western Travels*, XVIII, *Pattie's Personal Narrative, 1824–1830; Willard's Inland Trade with New Mexico, 1825, and Downfall of the Fredonian Republic; and Malte-Brun's Account of Mexico*, 93–94.

[22] Thwaites, *Early Western Travels*, IV, 133–134.

[23] Ibid., p. 137.

[24] Thwaites, *Early Western Travels*, X, *Hulme's Journal, 1818–19; Flower's Letters from Lexington and the Illinois, 1819; Flower's Letters from the Illinois, 1820–21; and Woods's Two Years' Residence, 1820–21*, 289.

[25] Shipman, *Frontier Life*, p. 28.

[26] Thwaites, *Early Western Travels*, XXII, *Part I of Maximilian,*

country was "alive with deer." As he rode through the area he scared up droves of fifty to a hundred animals. A resident said he had killed as many as six without moving from one spot. Other settlers said a professional hunter could kill fifteen hundred deer in a year.[27] A Texas traveler in the 1840's said that three or four fire-hunters could kill twenty or thirty deer in "a day or so."[28] Clearly, game was a major crop. The frontiersman gathered it with his rifle.

In the manner of any good tool, the muzzle-loading rifle was adaptable. Meat-getting was its principal job; occasionally it performed others. Fire was intimately a part of frontier living. If a man worked at night, he worked by the light of an open flame —from a campfire, a fireplace, a torch, a candle, or a lamp. He cooked with fire, dried meat with it, used it to clear land. He hollowed logs with fire. Without fire he was often helpless. His rifle was a handy firemaker. He prepared a pile of kindling, placed some tow and a few grains of powder in the pan of his empty rifle; he pulled the trigger to light the tow and dumped the coal onto the kindling. He huffed and puffed and had his fire.[29]

On the plains and prairies the frontiersman's dignity, if not his very life, depended upon keeping a horse handy. In desperate circumstances, he might capture a horse with his rifle. With strong prayer, a good eye, and a bundle of luck, he could crease

Prince of Wied's Travels in the Interior of North America, 1832–1834, 168.

[27] Andrew Forest Muir, ed., *Texas in 1837: An Anonymous, Contemporary Narrative* (Austin: University of Texas Press, 1958), p. 75.

[28] Hollon and Butler, *Bollaert's Texas,* p. 277.

[29] John G. W. Dillin, *The Kentucky Rifle,* 4th ed. (York, Pennsylvania: Trimmer Printing, Inc., 1959), pp. 57–58.

a wild horse. A western traveler in 1833 explained the art in these words: "It consists in shooting the horse in the neck with a single ball so as to graze his neck bone, and not to cut the pith of it."[30] The traveler saw a young hunter make such a shot. The horse fell to the ground stunned. Before it recovered, the hunter secured it with a lariat. In this case, the animal suffered no damage.[31] A hunter on Galveston Island in 1822 reported a similar success. His horse limped for a few days following capture but eventually recovered completely.[32] William Bollaert compiled a list of Texas hunting techniques of the 1840's. He says that wild-horse hunters creased mustangs in the woods, where roping was difficult.[33] In the 1820's Noah Smithwick and a friend set out to walk from Victoria, Texas, to a settlement on the Colorado River. On their way they passed drove after drove of mustangs. Exasperated at walking in the midst of so many horses, the friend took action. He killed a wild cow, plaited a rope from the hide, hid himself near a waterhole. When a band of horses came to drink, he creased one, ran forward, and tied it to a tree. He stood by for action. Nothing happened. The animal's neck was broken.[34] Most efforts at creasing ended in the same fashion. It was strictly an emergency technique.

A man with a steady stomach might occasionally use his rifle to get a drink of water. In 1822 a party of Santa Fe traders ran

[30] Thwaites, *Western Travels*, XXI, *Wyeth's Oregon, or a Short History of a Long Journey, 1832; and Townsend's Narrative of a Journey across the Rocky Mountains, 1834*, 87.

[31] Ibid.

[32] W. S. Lewis, "The Adventures of the 'Lively' Immigrants," *The Quarterly of the Texas State Historical Association*, III, No. 2 (October, 1899), 95–96.

[33] Hollon and Butler, *Bollaert's Texas*, p. 257.

[34] Smithwick, *Evolution of a State*, p. 23.

out of water between the Arkansas and Cimarron rivers. Thirst drove some of them to slit the ears of pack mules for blood. That merely increased their suffering. The strongest men fanned out ahead to hunt for water. Actually, they were nearer the Cimarron than they suspected. Several of them chanced upon a lone buffalo, fresh from the river, sluggish from drinking. They shot the animal, opened its stomach, strained off the water, and satisfied their thirst.[35] Buffalo hunters sometimes used the same technique simply to avoid a ride back to camp.[36]

Making fire, creasing horses, and getting water were incidental uses for the rifle, in the same category as signaling to friends or making a holiday noise. More important, the rifle furnished entertainment. In any culture, entertainment, recreation, and work shade into each other. An adaptable tool may serve all purposes. At the present time, the automobile is transportation for work or for pleasure. It is a laboratory for amateur mechanics, a billboard for satire and humor—not to mention stamps and permits. It is an arena for courtship, a status symbol. Its functions intermingle. So it was with the rifle on the frontier. An Ohio tourist in 1807 summed up the situation. A young woodsman hailed the writer's boat, wishing to work his way downriver to the falls. He wanted to attend a "gathering" there. The boatman described him: "He had his rifle with him and was prepared for any kind of frolick which might be going forward."[37] Fifteen years later, an Illinois resident would say of his neighbors: "They have but few diversions amongst them except

---

[35] Max L. Moorhead, ed., *Commerce of the Prairies by Josiah Gregg* (Norman: University of Oklahoma Press, 1954), pp. 14–15.

[36] Thwaites, *Early Western Travels*, XXI, 171–172.

[37] Ibid., IV, 136.

hunting and shooting."[38] The rifle went everywhere the people went.

A wedding, a log-rolling, a cabin-raising, or just a visit was an excuse to show off skill with the rifle, a chance to practice techniques. At an early date, American backwoodsmen acquired a reputation for keen shooting and a willingness to demonstrate. As the Second Continental Congress organized for war, John Adams wrote his dear Abigail of the skill of riflemen, saying, "They are the most accurate marksmen in the world."[39] He had seen some perform. Volunteer riflemen on their way to Boston had stopped to entertain the public in the towns along their route. On one occasion, two brothers performed for townsmen. One held a small board, five by seven inches, between his knees. In its center was a piece of paper the size of a silver dollar. His brother fired eight times from a distance of sixty yards and hit the target every time. Another man held a barrel stave alongside his body. A friend fired shot after shot into the stave from a distance of sixty yards.[40] The spectators were amazed.

Sixty years later, riflemen on their way to war would still stop to amaze the townspeople. In 1835 John Duval joined a Kentucky company to fight in the Anglo-Texan revolt against Mexico. The soldiers took a steamboat from Louisville to New Orleans. At every wood and freight stop on the river the volunteers went ashore to get up impromptu shooting matches with the

[38] Ibid., X, 318.

[39] Charles Francis Adams, *Familiar Letters of John Adams and His Wife Abigail Adams, During the Revolution. With a Memoir of Mrs. Adams* (New York: Hurd and Houghton, 1876), p. 66.

[40] *The Virginia Gazette, 1775*, quoted in Charles Winthrop Sawyer, *Firearms in American History: 1600–1800*, 2 vols. (Boston: Pimpton Press, 1910), I, 78–79.

natives. Duval writes that the riflemen could put three balls out of five into a dollar-sized target at a hundred yards.[41]

Among frontiersmen, shooting matches were common. Sometimes each shooter in a match paid an entry fee—the winner kept the pot. A tavern keeper might organize a turkey shoot. He tied a turkey behind a log so that only its head would be visible to shooters a hundred yards away. A man paid a fee for each shot he took. The one who killed the bird kept it for his prize.[42]

Squirrel hunts were sometimes organized as contests. Only the animals shot through the head counted. The head shot was a necessity as much as a test of skill. Most frontier rifles were larger than forty caliber in bore. A ball that size mutilated any small animal shot through the body, lacing the meat with splintered bone. Daniel Boone once showed John Audubon another technique for killing squirrels with a rifle. It required more skill than did the head shot. In most regions it was called barking off squirrels. Boone and Audubon walked to a stand of hardwood trees in a river bottom. Boone pointed out a squirrel in a tree some fifty paces away. He aimed for a spot just beneath the animal's body. When he fired, the ball shattered the bark, sending the squirrel flying through the air. The concussion killed it without leaving a mark on the carcass. Boone repeated the feat several times without moving from the spot. Audubon says that in his travels later he saw many other riflemen bark off squirrels.[43]

Fiction writers have been fascinated by the test of skill called driving the nail. They have had their heros perform the trick at

[41] John C. Duval, *Early Times in Texas* (Austin, Texas: H. P. N. Gammel & Co., 1892), pp. 14–15.

[42] Thwaites, *Early Western Travels*, IV, 33.

[43] Audubon, *Delineations*, pp. 60–61.

fantastic distances. In reality, the sport was popular among riflemen. A heavy backstop was selected—a post or tree would do.
A nail was driven about two-thirds its length into the backstop.
Sometimes a white background was painted around the nail.
Shooters usually stood thirty to forty yards from the target. The
object of the contest was to drive the nail the remaining distance
into the wood. Betting on the results was not unknown. Nicking
or bending the nail was a passing shot. It usually took a square
hit on the head to win. One observer of such a contest wrote that
one out of three shots drove the nail.[44] If nails were not available
—they were often scarce—shooters could try to thread the needle.
For this test, a hole was made in a board, or slab, slightly larger
than a rifle ball in diameter. Contestants lined up at any agree-
able distance and fired in order. The object was to put a ball
through the hole without touching the edge.[45]

The popularity of fire-hunting on the frontier led to tests for
skill in night shooting. Snuffing the candle served the purpose
admirably. It might be wise to remember that snuffing a candle
is not the same thing as snuffing *out* a candle. The snuff of a
candle is, of course, the charred portion of the wick. As the snuff
gets longer, the light dims, the flame turns red, the candle
smokes. With a pinch of thumb and finger, or with a snuffer,
the upper part of the wick is cut off. The flame whitens, gives
more light. For the shooting contest, a calm night was necessary.
The candle was placed on a stump, or block, with a man sta-
tioned to the side to tend it. The riflemen gathered forty or fifty

[44] Ibid., p. 60.
[45] Philip Henry Grosse, *Letters From Alabama (U.S.) Chiefly Relating to Natural History* (London, 1859), pp. 130–133, quoted in Frank
Lawrence Owsley, *Plain Folk of the Old South* (Baton Rouge: Louisiana
State University Press, 1949), p. 120.

yards away. A man took his shot when the watchman signaled that the snuff was long enough. A high shot missed completely; it might cause the flame to flicker. A low shot cut the wick or candle below the flame—a failure. The candle must be relit. A perfect shot passed through the center of the flame, cut off the snuff without putting out the light. When a man hit the mark, the flame flickered, then brightened noticeably. John Audubon saw a match in which one expert snuffed the candle three shots out of seven.[46]

In frontier literature, the list of games goes on—anything might serve as a target. Men who made their living with the rifle cherished it, were proud of their skill in its use. The rifle fed them, sometimes clothed them. It entertained them, earned them money. With his rifle a man could hold on, conquer time. The environment that nourished a frontier culture is gone. Few would welcome its return. An understanding of the culture—its meaning in the stream of American history—depends in part upon an understanding of the tools that built it. The muzzle-loading rifle was a magnificent tool. It was the common denominator of frontier living.

[46] Audubon, *Delineations*, p. 61.

FREDERICK JACKSON TURNER
AND WALTER PRESCOTT WEBB
Frontier Historians

BY RAY A. BILLINGTON

WHY DO WE RIGHTLY acclaim Frederick Jackson Turner and
Walter Prescott Webb as the greatest historians of the American
frontier? What elements in their intellects and training allowed
them to serve as architects for the bold historical edifices to
which most of us only add bricks and mortar? Or, to select a
more appropriate metaphor, what were the endowments that let
Frederick Jackson Turner and Walter Prescott Webb serve as
trail blazers into new frontiers of learning, while the rest of us
merely plod behind?

Each of these men advanced two new concepts that have altered
our understanding of the American past. Turner's famous essay,
"The Significance of the Frontier in American History," read
before the American Historical Association in 1893, held that
the imported institutions of the United States and the inherited
traits of its people had been slightly altered by the three-centuries-

long process of frontiering that was coming to an end at the close
of the century. Democracy, individualism, and nationalism were
strengthened, he suggested, while Americans were more mobile,
materialistic, inventive, and buoyant than their European cousins.[1]
Characteristically, Turner did little to prove his "frontier hypothesis," for by the early 1900's he was off on a fresh scent. As
people moved westward, he reasoned, they engulfed a succession
of physiographic provinces, each as large as a European kingdom,
and each differing in soil, climate, and natural resources. These
differences resulted in a nation of "sections," in which unique
economic activities created a demand for legislative programs
unsuited to the needs of other sections. Turner spent most of his
later life re-examining the history of the United States in terms
of this sectional hypothesis.[2]

Webb also advanced two fresh concepts. One he set forth in
his monumental book, *The Great Plains*; the area west of the
ninety-eighth meridian, he held, differed so markedly from the

[1] This essay was first printed in the *Proceedings of the Forty-First
Annual Meeting of the State Historical Society of Wisconsin* (Madison,
State Historical Society of Wisconsin, 1894), pp. 79–112, and a short
time later in the American Historical Association, *Annual Report for the
Year 1893* (Washington, Government Printing Office, 1894), pp. 192–
227. It has been often reprinted since, and is today most readily available in Frederick Jackson Turner, *The Frontier in American History*
(New York: Henry Holt & Co., 1920; paperback edition, New York:
Holt, Rinehart & Winston, 1962), pp. 1–38, and Ray A. Billington, ed.,
Frontier and Section: Selected Essays of Frederick Jackson Turner
(Englewood Cliffs, New Jersey: Prentice-Hall, 1961), pp. 36–62.

[2] Two books by Turner, both published posthumously, explain his
views on sectionalism. Interpretative essays are in Frederick Jackson
Turner, *The Significance of Sections in American History* (New York:
Henry Holt & Co., 1932), while *The United States, 1830–1850: The
Nation and Its Sections* (New York: Henry Holt & Co., 1935) examines one segment of the nation's history in sectional terms.

humid East that civilization was radically altered there. Men reared in traditions of the forest environment of Europe and the eastern United States must devise new weapons, new tools, new means of transportation, new attitudes, new forms of cultural expression. *The Great Plains* brilliantly detailed these changes, showing how the grasslands were conquered by the Colt revolver and barbed wire, and how the environment reshaped the cultural and behavioral patterns of its conquerors.[3] Webb's second contribution was the "boom hypothesis," advanced in memorable form in his book, *The Great Frontier*. The Western world, he argued, enjoyed a boom period between the age of discovery and the early twentieth century, as virgin lands were occupied in the Americas, in Australia, and throughout the world. During these years, man adjusted his institutions to expansion, enjoying the blessings of democracy, free enterprise, religious freedom, and legal systems designed to protect the individual from society. Webb reluctantly concluded that the end of the boom period doomed mankind to ever increasing social controls, and that historians of the future would look back on the period from 1500 to 1950 as an abnormal age that could never be repeated.[4]

These were challenging hypotheses—the "frontier" and "sectional" concepts of Turner, the "arid west" and "Great Frontier" theses of Webb. They have altered the study and teaching of American history. They have stirred usually placid historians into violent controversy. And they have stimulated more constructive

[3] Walter Prescott Webb, *The Great Plains* (Boston: Ginn and Company, 1931).

[4] Walter Prescott Webb, *The Great Frontier* (Boston: Houghton, Mifflin, 1952).

effort on the part of scholars than any interpretations of American history advanced in the past century, with the possible sole
exception of Charles Beard's economic interpretation.

Whence came these startling concepts? What mutual experiences, what common manner of training, what natural endowments, did Turner and Webb share that allowed them to pioneer
so boldly on new intellectual frontiers? There is no simple answer to these questions, but we can isolate a number of instances
that reveal a surprising similarity between the background and
training of the two men, and that show their temperaments to be
comparable.

To begin at the beginning, as is proper for historians, both
were influenced by the primitive environment in which they
were reared. The world of the youthful Fred Turner was a
frontier world. The town of Portage, Wisconsin, where he was
born in 1861, boasted fewer than three thousand inhabitants at
the time, and only a thousand more twenty years later. Everywhere were evidences of an emerging society—Winnebago Indian villages on the nearby Baraboo River, great lumber rafts
on the Wisconsin River, a stream of new arrivals from Europe
and the East to the newly cleared farm lands of Columbia
County.[5] All of this Turner remembered vividly. He wrote to
Carl Becker in 1925:

I have poled down the Wisconsin in a dugout with Indian guides
from "Grandfather Bull Falls," through virgin forests of balsam
firs, seeing deer in the river,—antlered beauties who watched us come
down with curious eyes then broke for the tall timber,—hearing the

[5] An account of frontier conditions in Portage during Turner's boyhood is in Ray A. Billington, "Young Fred Turner," *Wisconsin Magazine of History*, XLVI (Autumn, 1962), 38–48.

squaws in their village on the high bank talk with their low treble to the bass of our Indian polesman,—feeling that I belonged to it all. I have seen a lynched man hanging from a tree when I came home from school in Portage, have played around old Fort Winnebago at its outskirts, have seen the red shirted Irish raftsmen *take* the town when they tied up and came ashore, have plodded up the "pinery" road that ran past our house to the pine woods of Northern Wisconsin, have seen Indians come in on their ponies to buy paint and ornaments and sell their furs; have stumbled on their camp on the Baraboo, where dried pumpkins were hung up, and cooking muskrats were in the kettle, and an Indian family were bathing in the river— the frontier in that sense, you see, was real to me, and when I studied history I did not keep my personal experiences in a water tight compartment away from my studies.[6]

If Turner's experiences in the forests of Wisconsin inclined him toward an interest in frontiers, so did those of Webb on the semiarid plains of West Texas. There he was reared, on a farm in wind-swept Stephens County, where his family settled when he was only four years old. Like Turner, he later recalled his boyhood as it influenced his later career:

A friend asked me once when I began preparation to write *The Great Plains*. I answered that I began at the age of four when my father left the humid east and set his family down in West Texas, in the very edge of the open, arid country which stretched north and west farther than a boy could imagine. There I touched the hem of the garment of the real frontier; there I tasted alkali. I was not the first man, or boy; but the first men, Indian fighters, buffalo hunters, trail-

[6] Turner to Carl Becker, December 16, 1925, Frederick Jackson Turner Papers, Henry E. Huntington Library, TU Box 34. Hereafter cited as Turner Papers, HM. Material from the Turner Papers is reproduced by permission of The Huntington Library, San Marino, California.

drivers, half-reformed outlaws, and Oklahoma boomers were all around, full of memories and eloquent in relating them to small boys. There I saw the crops burned by drought, eaten by grasshoppers, and destroyed by hail. I felt the searing winds come furnace-hot from the desert to destroy in a day the hopes of a year, and I saw a trail herd blinded and crazy from thirst completely out of control of horse-weary cowboys with faces so drawn they looked like death masks. In the hard-packed yard and on the encircling red-stone hills was the geology, in the pasture the desert botany and all the wild animals of the plains save the buffalo. The Indians, the fierce Comanches, had so recently departed, leaving memories so vivid and tales so harrowing that their red ghosts, lurking in every motte and hollow, drove me home all prickly with fear when I ventured too far. The whole great plains was there in microcosm, and the book I wrote was but an extension and explanation of what I had known firsthand in minia-ture, in a sense an autobiography with scholarly trimmings.[7]

The lesson to be distilled from these two boyhood experiences is clear. Turner and Webb, in propounding their historical views, were merely translating into theory a world with which they were all too familiar. Turner not only knew but *understood* the Mississippi Valley frontier; Webb *felt* the aridity of the Great Plains as part of his learning experience. Each could apply that understanding to his theorizing; neither could have done so if reared in a different environment.

But when Webb referred to *The Great Plains* as "an autobi-ography with scholarly trimmings," he was referring to another

[7] Walter Prescott Webb, "History as High Adventure," *American Historical Review*, LXIV (January, 1959), 273–274. This, and other lectures and essays, are conveniently reprinted in Walter Prescott Webb, *An Honest Preface and Other Essays* (Boston: Houghton, Mifflin, 1959).

facet of his preparation—one that he shared with Turner. Neither received the formal training in his special subject that would be expected of the graduate student of today. Turner, it is true, graduated from the University of Wisconsin in 1884, won a Master of Arts degree from that institution three years later, and earned his doctorate at the Johns Hopkins University in 1890. He was also fortunate enough to study under a great master at Wisconsin, William Francis Allen, who taught him to use sources critically, to view society as an evolving organism, and to apply the principles of multiple causation to all problems. But Allen was a medievalist, and lived in a day when all teaching was governed by Edward A. Freeman's dictum that "history is past politics, and politics is present history." So Turner was immersed in the institutional history of the Middle Ages, but his formal training in American history was limited to one course for one-third of a year. "I had," he wrote later, "a lack of general American history training which in some ways was a handicap—requiring much hard work on my part—but which in other ways was an advantage in that I hadn't been fitted into the mould of the teachers of the usual successive courses in American history. I had to work out my own salvation."[8]

Walter Webb had to work out his own salvation as well. His educational career was as haphazard as Turner's was orthodox, for schools and money were unfamiliar commodities in West Texas in those days, but he managed to graduate from the University of Texas at the age of twenty-seven. High-school teaching seemed his destiny until the university needed a historian to drum history into would-be teachers, and in 1918 Webb was added to

[8] Turner to Merle Curti, August 8, 1928, Turner Papers, HM, TU Box 39.

its staff. The doctorate was acquired some years later (after Harvard had refused him admission as a graduate student) when his colleagues persuaded him to submit his first published book, *The Great Plains*, as a dissertation. Had he been admitted to Harvard, and studied there under Turner, Webb might have become a parrot rather than a prophet, a disciple rather than a master. Instead he was free to shape his own ideas. "I was," he later recalled, "excellently prepared [to become a Western historian] because I had never had a course in that field, and therefore could view it without preconceived notions or borrowed points of view."[9]

This is not to suggest that the only road to eminence is lack of training, or that would-be historians should avoid history courses. It is to suggest that brilliant minds can, on occasion, be shackled and that deep-seated enthusiasms can be stifled by too much immersion in discipline. Both Webb and Turner escaped this, and hence were endowed with an enthusiasm for historical studies that lasted through their lifetimes. This enthusiasm, this passion for the subject, this fanatical belief in history, was another ingredient in the receipt for greatness that they shared.

Young Fred Turner discovered the excitement of historical study when he was a graduate student, spending his hours in the State Historical Society Library as he prepared his masters' thesis. "The more I dip into American history," he wrote his fiancee in the fall of 1887, "the more I can see what a great field there is here for a life study. One must even specialize here. I think I shall spend my study chiefly upon the Northwest and more generally on the Mississippi Valley. The history of this country remains to

9 Webb, "History as High Adventure," p. 272.

be written."[10] Six months later he was still filled with enthusiasm. "I do not talk anything now but Western history," he wrote. ". . . I have taken a fever of enthusiasm over the possibilities of the great west and of the magnificent scope of United States history in general."[11] A year later, now at Johns Hopkins University, his enthusiasm was still mounting. "I am in the full swing of university life and I *like* it," he wrote. "I am becoming to feel like a boy let *out* of school,—I really wish to jump and shout aloud in the new freedom and happiness of having pleasant work and *only* pleasant work. I am growing like a plant in the sunshine."[12] There spoke a zealot, and that zeal burned through Turner's lifetime. Understanding the past was not only an exciting experience beyond parallel, but the key to a better life and a better world.

Walter Prescott Webb shared those views. To him, history was the great persuader, capable of bending men's views and shaping the type of society that he desired. On the very night that Webb heard of the Supreme Court's decision invalidating a major New Deal agency that he approved of, the National Recovery Administration, he began work on a book of protest. *Divided We Stand* resulted, a harsh little volume that offended more people than it pleased. Again, in 1963, just before his death, he withdrew as author of a major volume in the New American Nation Series to begin a book that would teach the South its economic progress was assured if it did not become entangled in the racial struggle.[13] "I wanted to write," he told an

[10] Turner to Caroline Mae Sherwood, September 5, 1887, Turner Papers, HM, TU Box B.

[11] Turner to Caroline Mae Sherwood, March 25, 1888, ibid., Box C.

[12] Turner to Caroline Mae Sherwood, October 12, 1888, ibid., Box D.

[13] Biographical information on Walter Prescott Webb is delightfully

audience of historians on one occasion, "so that people could understand me; I wanted to persuade them, lure them along from sentence to paragraph, make them see patterns of truth in the kaleidoscope of the past, exercise upon them the marvelous magic of words as conveyors of thought."[14] Neither Webb nor Turner was a half-time historian, content to confine the subject to the classroom or study desk. To those men, history was a continuous inspiration, a source of unending pleasure, and a magic talisman in the evolution of a better world. Their unquestioning belief in their subject aided them as they groped toward the fresh ideas that are associated with their names.

Yet neither was a prolific writer—and here is another ingredient in the receipt for greatness. Turner wrote one book during his lifetime, together with some two-score articles and a handful of reviews. The idea underlying *The Great Plains* struck Webb in the 1920's, but not until 1931 did the book appear. *The Texas Rangers* was published in 1935, eighteen years after it was begun. He and his seminars labored for fourteen years to produce *The Great Frontier*. Judged by modern academic standards, which assign a major place to quantity in a publish-or-perish world, neither man was successful, and probably would be assigned to a perpetual role as associate professor. Walter Webb realized this. "You fellows," he told his younger colleagues late in his life, "never *would* have hired me. And if you *had* hired me, you wouldn't have kept me. And if you *had* kept me, you wouldn't

---

presented by Joe B. Frantz in "An Appreciative Introduction," in Webb, *An Honest Preface and Other Essays*, pp. 3–58, and in "Walter Prescott Webb," in Wilbur R. Jacobs, John W. Caughey, and Joe B. Frantz, *Turner, Bolton, and Webb* (Seattle: University of Washington Press, 1965), pp. 75–102.

[14] Webb, "History as High Adventure," p. 268.

have promoted me. I came along at the last possible moment to have made good in this profession."[15] Webb also half-seriously believed that he could not have succeeded outside Texas, where, as he once told a friend, "we sit on our tails . . . and swell up to inordinate size if we write one book."[16] There, "nobody told me I ought to produce, write articles, get into print whether I had anything to say or not."[17]

Yet Turner, and probably Webb, despite his denials, desperately wanted to write. Throughout his lifetime, Turner planned exciting projects—monographs, biographies, regional studies, textbooks—and often he signed contracts agreeing to produce them. Repeatedly he sought to carry one or the other of these projects to a conclusion, and always he failed. The textbook that was to revolutionize college teaching and enrich its author never advanced beyond the third chapter. Others died a-borning. The volume on which he spent his last thirty years, *The United States, 1830–1850*, was unfinished at his death in 1932, and his closest friend believed that it would never have been finished, if Turner had lived forever.[18]

The truth is that neither man possessed a temperament that would allow a regular period of writing each day, no matter what the distractions. Instead, both seemed to create distractions.

---

[15] Frantz, "Walter Prescott Webb," in Jacobs, Caughey, and Frantz, *Turner, Bolton, and Webb*, p. 101.

[16] Frantz, "An Appreciative Introduction," *An Honest Preface and Other Essays*, p. 46.

[17] Walter Prescott Webb, "The Historical Seminar," *Mississippi Valley Historical Review*, XLII (June, 1955), 21–22.

[18] Turner's difficulties in writing are described in Ray A. Billington, "Why Some Historians Rarely Write History: A Case Study of Frederick Jackson Turner," *Mississippi Valley Historical Review*, L (June, 1963), 3–27.

Turner was forever writing letters, chatting with friends, re-working his classroom lectures, paddling a canoe on Lake Men-dota or the Charles River, escaping into the North Woods, or, when supposedly working, spending his time drawing maps, clip-ping newspapers for his bulging files, or pasting together scrap-books on subjects that caught his fancy. Webb never missed his weekly afternoon with the *Saturday Evening Post* or his cover-to-cover reading of the *U.S. News and World Report.* More often than not, he could be found at the Headliners Club, which he founded, cup of coffee in hand, or driving two hundred miles in an afternoon for a conversation with a friend who had some-thing to say. Webb spent hours building the herd of Santa Ger-trudis cattle on his ranch near Austin, or engaging in remarkably profitable real estate deals.[19] "It's hell," he once said, "to be lazy and ambitious at the same time."[20]

Actually neither was lazy, and when inspiration stirred them—when, in other words, they felt that an idea was worth expressing —they worked furiously. Turner's intervals of writing were so passionately intense that they endangered his health. "Whenever I tried to go ahead under full steam," he explained to his pub-lisher, "—and this is the way I write most effectively—for I must write passionately if I do it well and originally—(I am not able to sit down to so many hundred words a day as a regular accomplishment)—whenever, I say, I have tried to really *push* ahead I have landed in the hospital."[21] Webb left no similar tes-timony concerning his working habits, but one of his colleagues

[19] Frantz, "An Appreciative Introduction," *An Honest Preface and Other Essays,* pp. 12, 24.

[20] Ibid., p. 46.

[21] Turner to Henry Holt & Company, April 5, 1921, Henry Holt & Company Archives, Princeton University Library, Folder F. J. Turner.

recorded the change that came over him when he was ready to write. "By nine o'clock in the morning the rapid two-fingered clack of his typewriter comes floating out of Garrison Hall 102, to be halted only by someone with a problem or an invitation to coffee. At eleven o'clock that night the typewriter will still be going as strong as ever in the now-still Garrison Hall. His pace is steady, never hurried, never impatient. His application is a marvel to his younger colleagues, who yield to a weariness that he never seems to feel."[22]

The lessons to be learned from this testimony are obvious. The tradition-shattering concepts that spell progress in history—or any other discipline—often come from the slow producers rather than from the highly motivated professionals whose assembly-line tactics result in a parade of books and articles. Men who take time to think may be branded as lazy in today's world, but some-times as much can be accomplished with feet on a desk as with fingers on a typewriter. To read leisurely and widely, to distill the experiences of past authors into personalized terms, to ponder these thoughts in unhurried fashion, this is to set in motion the creative process. If Turner and Webb had been less afflicted with what the world judges as faults, they would not have known the date with destiny that has been their lot.

Yet their very virtues doomed them to produce the most diffi-cult—and least lucrative—form of historical writing. Both knew and admired the great narrative historians whose works captured the popular imagination. Turner, for example, was intensely fond of Francis Parkman's stirring prose. "He has," Turner wrote as a graduate student, "a delightful style, abounding in

[22] Frantz, "An Appreciative Introduction," *An Honest Preface and Other Essays*, p. 11.

metaphor—and smooth flowing, but best of all he tells his story
with as much fascination for the reader as if it were a novel—No,
with more fascination, for I never could feel the interest in a
novel I do in real history well told."[23] Walter Webb shared this
taste. Once, deploring the wooden style of the twenty-four–
volume Old American Nation Series, he complained that in those
books there was "none of the savage beauty of Parkman, the
insight of Macauley, the vision of Gibbon, or the restrained yet
voluminous imagination of Jules Michelet, of whom James West-
fall Thompson once said: 'He not only took history for life, he
lived himself into the past to an extent unexcelled before or
since.' "[24] Turner and Webb longed to write narrative history,
and Webb proved that he could do so with his story of the Texas
Rangers. Yet both turned their backs on this tempting field to
produce the thoughtful analytical studies for which they are
known, studies that explore not *what* man did but *why*. Their
concern was not with the puppets who danced on the world's
stage, but with the forces that manipulated the strings. "It is in
narrative history," wrote Turner at one time, "that I am least
experienced or (I fear) competent. . . . My strength, or weakness,
lies in interpretation, correlation, elucidation of large tendencies
to bring out new points of view and in giving a new setting. . . .
I am not a good saga-man."[25] So he was not, and he watched
in envy as less-gifted historians produced the broadly landscaped
chronicles or well-paying textbooks that captured popular inter·

[23] Turner to Caroline Mae Sherwood, September 2, 1887, Turner
Papers, HM, TU Box B.
[24] Webb, *An Honest Preface and Other Essays*, pp. 149–150.
[25] Turner to Henry Holt & Company, April 5, 1921, Henry Holt &
Company Archives, Princeton University, Folder F. J. Turner.

est and eased the financial strains to which he was subjected during his lifetime.

It is clear that Turner and Webb shared many experiences in common, and that these helped to shape the nature of their historical interests. But are these sufficient to explain their greatness? Other historians were wise enough to build theories from their own observations. Others were inadequately trained in their discipline, were gloriously enthralled by the study of history, and stressed analytical rather than narrative history. Others—though all too few—were more concerned with quality than quantity. Yet none among these produced original concepts that revolutionized our understanding of the past, as did Turner and Webb. What, then, was the secret of their success?

The answer to this question is more easily stated than proven. Turner and Webb were endowed by nature to respond creatively to an external stimulus. To explain this obscure statement is to venture into the hazy area of the psychology of creativity. Students of this subject believe that fresh ideas are the product of a long period of gestation. They tell us that in all problem solving we gradually accumulate pertinent information, rejecting what is nonessential and retaining in our minds what may prove useful; we also test and either keep or discard haphazard ideas as they occur. As we dwell longer and longer with the subject, the subconscious continually generates flashes of insight, even though the problem has been laid aside consciously. Then, suddenly and accidentally, we stumble on a single bit of information that brings the whole solution into focus. This psychologists call the "A-HA" experience. Not all people are capable of recognizing the obscure fact that triggers this burst of illumination; those who do so are the geniuses of the world.[26]

Both Turner and Webb could recognize such a stimulus. In Turner's case, we may trace the evolution of the frontier concept in his mind by reading the notes that he left behind. We know that he became interested in the movement of pioneers westward even as a graduate student, and that this interest was accentuated in 1891 and 1892 as he began his teaching career at the University of Wisconsin. The course on constitutional and political history of the United States, which he had inherited, was quickly discarded for one on economic and social history, this in turn was focused more and more on the westward movement. "Particular attention," students were told in the fall of 1892, "will be paid to the spread of settlement across the continent."[27] Turner was also compelled to think about the frontier by a course of extension lectures he was preparing at this time on the colonization of North America. These were new subjects, untouched by the textbooks, and their preparation meant a vast amount of haphazard reading in a wide variety of materials. Statistical volumes must be mastered to trace the course of expansion—volumes such as Francis A. Walker's *Statistical Atlas of the United States*. Foreign travelers who had visited the American West must be read for their descriptions of the settlements. These visitors commented on the differences between ways of life and thought in East and

[26] Views of psychologists on creative thinking may be examined in such books as: Robert Thomson, *The Psychology of Thinking* (Baltimore: Penguin Books, 1959), and Donald McEwen Johnson, *The Psychology of Thought and Judgment* (New York: Harper, 1955).

[27] *Catalogue of the University of Wisconsin* (Madison, 1891), pp. 114–116; (Madison, 1892), pp. 97–99; (Madison, 1893), pp. 61–62.

West, and to understand these, social theorists must be consulted, scholars such as Achille Loria and Walter Bagehot. So Turner read, in books and magazines and reviews, keeping fragmentary notes on tiny pieces of paper that allow us to retrace his trail.[28]

We can only speculate on what he was reading when the burst of insight—the "A-HA" experience—flooded his mind with the frontier hypothesis. Probably it was the bulky *Compendium of the Eleventh Census: 1890*, which arrived at the State Historical Society Library in 1892. Naturally he would turn to the usual essay, "The Progress of the Nation," and there his eyes would fall on the now-famous words: "Up to and including 1890 the country had a frontier of settlement, but at present the unsettled area has been so broken into by isolated bodies of settlement that there can hardly be said to be a frontier line."[29] We can only wonder what thoughts flashed through his mind as he read. Did he ask himself how the frontier had helped shape American civilization during its three-centuries-long existence? Did he ponder on the changes that would alter the nation's culture in the post-frontier era? We will never know the answer to these questions, but we do know that only a few months later he penned an essay, "Problems in American History," which advanced the

[28] For an excellent discussion of the influence of these and other statistical works on Turner, see Fulmer Mood, "The Development of Frederick Jackson Turner as a Historical Thinker," Colonial Society of Massachusetts, *Transactions, 1937–1942*, XXXIV (Boston, 1943), 283–352. Ray A. Billington, *America's Frontier Heritage* (New York: Holt, Rinehart, and Winston, 1966), pp. 8–12, deals briefly with Turner's reading at the time and other influences that helped shape his theory.

[29] United States Bureau of the Census, 11th Census, 1890, *Compendium of the Eleventh Census: 1890. Part I, Population* (Washington, 1892), p. xlviii.

hypothesis in skeleton form, and before the year was out he had a rough draft written of his more famous work, "The Significance of the Frontier in American History."[30]

Walter Webb enjoyed a similar experience when he happened upon the arid American West concept, which he advanced in *The Great Plains*. But, unlike Turner, he remembered the circumstances and the thrill of the moment. His period of intellectual gestation occurred during the years spent in reading about the Texas Rangers. While thus engaged, he was asked by an oil company to prepare a series of articles on the Rangers for a promotional magazine it was launching, and readily succumbed when he was promised two cents a word. As he arranged his material and started to write, a flash of insight suddenly brought the whole problem into focus. He later recalled:

The idea came to me on a dark winter night when a heavy rain was rattling on the roof of the small back room where I was trying to write an article for the oil magazine. By this time I knew a great deal about the Texas Rangers, their dependence on horses, and their love of the Colt revolver; I knew the nature of their enemies, primarily the Comanches, and I knew the kind of society they represented and defended. I was ready for that moment of synthesis that comes after long hours of aimless research to give understanding and animation to inert knowledge. What I saw that night was that when Stephen F. Austin brought his colonists to Texas, he brought them to the edge of one environment, the Eastern woodland, and to the border of another environment, the Great Plains. The Texas Rangers were

[30] "Problems in American History," was first published in the undergraduate newspaper at the University of Wisconsin, *The Aegis*, VII (November 4, 1892), 48–52. It has been reprinted in Frederick Jackson Turner, *The Early Writings of Frederick Jackson Turner* (Madison: University of Wisconsin Press, 1938), pp. 71–83, and in Billington, ed., *Frontier and Section*, pp. 28–36.

called into existence and kept in existence primarily to defend the settlements against Indians on horseback, Indians equipped with weapons that could be used on horseback. These Texans, fresh from the forests, had no such weapons, for theirs had been developed in the woods and were not suitable for horsemen. While the conflict between the Rangers and the Comanches was at its height, Samuel Colt invented the revolver, the ideal weapon for a man on horseback. It took a year to gather the proof of what I knew that night, and I knew that something very important happened when the American people emerged from the woodland and undertook to live on the plains. In that transition the Texans were the forerunners, the Rangers the spearhead of the advance, and the revolver an adaptation to the needs of a new situation.

The excitement of that moment was probably the greatest creative sensation I have ever known.[31]

Both Turner and Webb were a long way from proving their theories when they experienced the flash of revelation that gave meaning to their reading and thought. Each had, in effect, evolved an imperfect and unproven hypothesis—Turner that Europeans were Americanized by their contact with the wilderness on the advancing frontier, Webb that the transformation was particularly complete in the arid West where, as he later put it, the environment was "an overwhelming force which has made man and his institutions bend to its imperious influence."[32] Now proof must be added, and each was off on an exciting quest that was to stretch over many years.

In this pursuit, both Turner and Webb displayed another characteristic that helps to explain their eminence. For each

[31] Webb, "History as High Adventure," pp. 270–271.
[32] Walter Prescott Webb in *The Westerners Brand Book*, XVI (Chicago: The Westerners, Chicago Corral, January, 1960), 81.

proved his ability to trample disciplinary range lines; both were
capable of breaking the barriers that departmentalize academic
thinking for most mortals. They showed their vision by borrow-
ing tools that they needed, from whatever area of learning. Today
we speak glibly of interdisciplinary approaches to many problems,
yet few of us are bold enough, or intelligent enough, to practice
what we preach. In their generation, Turner and Webb were
reckless innovators who flew in the face of all tradition.

Fortunately, each was equipped by training and instinct to do
so. The one professor at The University of Texas who made a
lasting impression on Webb was Lindley Miller Keasbey, a
European-trained student of institutional history who borrowed
freely from economics, anthropology, and sociology. Webb later
remembered that it was "Keasbey who gave me an understanding
for and an appreciation of the relationships between an environment and the civilization resting upon it; it was Keasbey who
taught me, and many others, to begin with the geology or geography, and build upon this foundation the superstructure of the
flora, fauna, and anthropology, arriving at last at the modern
civilization growing out of this foundation."[33] This was the same
logical progression that he followed in testing his Great Plains
hypothesis. He studied geology, climatology, botany, and anthropology. He mastered a knowledge of the Indian cultures that
thrived there. He taught himself technological details to appreciate the role of the Colt revolver and barbed wire. He read
widely in law to trace the changes in legal institutions governing
land, water, and mineral rights in a semiarid area. He studied
literary and religious works to understand the alterations of cul-

[33] Webb, "History as High Adventure," p. 279.

tural patterns beyond the ninety-eighth meridian. These were boldly imaginative tasks, yet they bore a rich reward. "I have," Webb later remembered, "never worked so hard or with such elation as in those days when I carved out the books piece after piece and found that they all fit together to form a harmonious pattern which I knew before hand was there."[34]

Turner's task was more difficult, partly because the social sciences were less well developed in his day, partly because historians were so aware of the prestigious antiquity of their own discipline that they showed little respect for others. Yet only by tapping the store of information accumulated in a variety of fields could he hope to explain the interrelationship between man and nature on the advancing frontier. He wrote many years later:

It became clear to me almost from the beginning that the advance of settlement required a study of the Atlantic coast sections and an understanding of their makeup—their people, institutions and ideas; and an understanding of the geographic provinces into which they moved—the new environments and conditions which modified these colonists as well as the contributions which the colonists made. Thus I had to have some knowledge of American physiography, I had to know something of demography, as well, and I had to recognize that these changes and inter-relations affected American social life and characteristics in general: its literature, art, religion, ideals.[35]

Once Turner recognized this, the whole spectrum of human studies opened before him; he read so widely that his friends twitted him by asking if he really were a historian or had deserted to another discipline. His pat answer could serve as a model for

[34] Ibid., p. 273.
[35] Turner to Merle Curti, August 8, 1928, Turner Papers, HM, TU Box 39.

all of us: "It is the subject that I am interested in, and I don't particularly care what name I bear."[36]

This completes our catalogue of characteristics shared by Frederick Jackson Turner and Walter Prescott Webb, although the list might be extended. But we must ask one further question if we are to appreciate the extent of their similarities. If a person exhibits the genius they displayed—if a historian dedicates himself to the study of an area with which he has been familiar since childhood, if he avoids contamination by refusing contact with college professors in his field, if he takes such irrational pleasure in his subject that he deprives himself of most of life's rewards, if he ignores the publish-or-perish dictum to concentrate on a very few publications of genuine significance, if he resists the temptation to write narrative history, if he is so naturally gifted that he can distill from his reading a completely new interpretation of the past, and if he possesses the intellectual boldness to master a variety of fields of knowledge in proving his hypotheses —if one boasts such a galaxy of talents as these, what are likely to be the rewards? The answer is fame and recognition, of course; both Turner and Webb were showered with honors from some of their contemporaries, including the presidency of the American Historical Association. But the answer is also disbelief, ridicule, and even abuse from others. Intellectual pioneers, it would seem, must suffer no less than pioneers on the Great Plains.

Fortunately for Turner, the principal attacks on him and his ideas were mounted after his death in 1932. By this time, the Great Depression had created a climate unsuitable to his views.

[36] Turner to Luther L. Bernard, November 24, 1928, ibid., TU Box 40.

In a world where internationalism rather than nationalism held the key to mankind's survival, where cooperation rather than individualism promised relief from economic chaos, where industrial-urban problems were of such magnitude that they bore little relationship to the rural past, the frontier thesis seemed woefully wrong. So the assault began, as young historian after young historian gained fame by beating Turner's bones in reviews, articles, and books. Some leaped on his statement of the thesis, charging him with inadequate definitions, inexact language, implausible analysis, and insufficient evidence. Others questioned the thesis itself, holding that neither a move westward nor a changed environment significantly altered man's behavior, and arguing that democracy, nationalism, individualism, and other allegedly "frontier" traits were European importations. Seldom has the tide of criticism run so strongly against any individual as it did against Turner in the 1930's and 1940's.[37]

Walter Webb suffered somewhat the same fate, but had the additional misfortune of living through the era of attack. Perhaps the most disagreeable event of his lifetime occurred when the Social Science Research Council selected his *The Great Plains* for appraisal as an outstanding contribution to historical literature. A critic was chosen to prepare an analysis of the book, to be followed by a conference of outstanding historians, who would discuss and evaluate the findings. Unhappily, the critic selected was Professor Fred A. Shannon of the University of Illinois, widely known for the acidity of his judgment and the bite of his tongue. Having spent the summer in a searching analysis of *The Great Plains*, he confronted Webb in the fall of 1939. The result was

37 For an analysis of this criticism see Ray A. Billington, *The American Frontier*, 2nd ed. (Washington, 1965), pp. 2–33.

tragedy. Webb, justly resentful of the uncourteous way in which
Shannon's criticisms were voiced, simply refused to reply, holding that his thesis was misunderstood. With emotions high and
tempers raw, with attention focused on trivial details rather than
on constructive suggestions, the conference accomplished little
save to wound Webb deeply.[38]

He was to pay for his originality again when *The Great Frontier* was published. Once more, popular reviewers were inclined
to look with favor on the book, and, once more, professional
critics sharpened their lances for a bitter assault. "In 'The Great
Frontier,' " one proclaimed, "Professor Webb of the University
of Texas reduces the frontier conception to its ultimate absurdity.
. . . It will not be profitable in such a review as this to call attention to the errors of fact, the ambiguous definitions, the dubi-
ous interpretations in which the book abounds. It will be enough
to indicate the fatal weakness in Webb's central conception of
the great frontier."[39] Added another in the *American Historical
Review*: "To be forced to say of a man who has written so well
that he has simply wasted his time in producing his most recent
book affords the reviewer no satisfaction but only discomfort and
regret. Unfortunately in writing *The Great Frontier* our Homer
did not merely nod; he stumbled in his sleep."[40] These were harsh

---

[38] Fred A. Shannon's "Appraisal" is printed in Fred A. Shannon, *An
Appraisal of Walter Prescott Webb's The Great Plains: A Study in
Institutions and Environment* (New York: Social Science Research
Council, 1940), pp. 3–112. Webb's comments on Shannon's critique are
in ibid., pp. 112–135, and the transcript of the discussion that followed
in ibid., pp. 139–213.

[39] Oscar Handlin, Review of *The Great Frontier*, by Walter Prescott
Webb, *The Nation* CLXXVI (January 10, 1953), 34.

[40] J. R. Hexter, Review of *The Great Frontier*, by Walter Prescott
Webb, *American Historical Review*, LVIII (July, 1953), 963.

words, and they were echoed in a disturbingly large number of reviews.

And they hurt. Turner was deeply stung by the two attacks on his frontier thesis launched before his death, yet refused to take up the cudgels in his own defense. "If," he wrote of one of the critics, "he is correct in his strictures on the conception of the frontier as a fundamental factor in American history, a whole lot of rather able men have been misled by it; and if the frontier conception has real value such men should be able to make any defense that may be called for."[41] Webb reacted in much the same way, holding that his thesis was valid and would stand despite the carping of critics. "*The Great Plains*," he told members of the American Historical Association in his presidential address before that body, "has never been revised, never will be revised by me, never has been imitated, and I am told by the publisher it never will go out of print."[42] So much, Webb was saying in effect, for picayunish sniping at a great book.

And Webb was right. He and Turner dealt in monumental ideas, in concepts that challenged traditional patterns of thought. Neither could be judged by the canons of judgment applicable to ordinary men. When Webb replied to one of his critics by saying, "I have never asserted that *The Great Plains* is history. . . . To me *The Great Plains* is a work of art," he spoke for all men of creative genius who operate on the borderlands of speculative thought.[43] One of Turner's staunch friends voiced the same belief to those who had assembled for the banquet marking his

[41] Turner to Frederick Merk, January 9, 1931, Turner Papers, HM, TU Box 45.

[42] Webb, "History as High Adventure," p. 274.

[43] Shannon, *Appraisal*, p. 114.

retirement from Harvard University in 1924. "Turner," said the friend, ". . . was a very great artist. He conceived the pageant of our national history in a new way and recorded it in new colors. It convinced scholars, not through the process of reason, but in precisely the same way a great novel or a great picture is called convincing."[44]

Turner and Webb were artists in the finest sense of the word. They were creative, and all creators face the wrath of those whose traditionalism they challenge. And, like all creators, they advanced concepts that were basically true but that would require generations for proper testing and proof. Today's generation of historians is again subjecting the frontier hypothesis to thoughtful examination, not in a spirit of complete adulation or rejection, but to test its truth. There is little doubt that, a generation hence, Walter Webb's *The Great Plains* will still be read with appreciation, and that *The Great Frontier* will be recognized as one of the most significant books of our time.

[44] Allyn A. Young to Carl Becker, October 9, 1925, Turner Papers, HM, TU Box 34A.